TEACHING   TEACHING

TEACHING SERIES

General Editor: Professor E. C. Wragg

Teaching Modern Languages   David Webb

in preparation

Teaching Art   John Lancaster and Ron George
Teaching Geography   Patrick Bailey
Teaching Mixed-Ability Groups   E. C. Wragg (editor)

TEACHING TEACHING

E. C. WRAGG

Professor of Education
University of Nottingham

DAVID & CHARLES
NEWTON ABBOT   LONDON
NORTH POMFRET (VT)   VANCOUVER

ISBN 0 7153 6858 3

© E. C. Wragg 1974

Set in 11 on 13pt Times
and printed in Great Britain
by John Sherratt and Son Ltd
Altrincham for David & Charles
(Holdings) Limited South Devon House
Newton Abbot Devon

Published in the United States of America
by David & Charles Inc North Pomfret
Vermont 05053 USA

Published in Canada by Douglas David &
Charles Limited 3645 McKechnie Drive
West Vancouver BC

Contents

List of Illustrations

Preface

'It is a serious indictment of the profession, however, to hear so many education instructors say that their students will appreciate what they are learning *after* they have had some practical teaching experience. What hurts is the obvious hypocrisy of making this statement and then giving a lecture on the importance of presenting material in such a way that the immediate needs and interests of the pupils are taken into consideration. Such instances reveal a misunderstanding of theory and practice. To be understood, concepts in education must be efficiently conceptualised to gain insight. With most present practices, the gorge between theory and practice grows deeper and wider, excavated by the very individuals who are pledged to fill it.'[1]

This criticism of American teacher training in 1963 by Ned Flanders is a useful starting point. A considerable amount of the discontent with teacher training procedures expressed by teachers, students and teacher trainers themselves stems from their dislike of the apparent gulf between theory and practice. At its worst it produces a lecture course saturated with information about historical, psychological, sociological and philosophical aspects of education, followed by an intensive burst of teaching practice in which the student is too desperately immersed in the intoxicating task of survival to stop and deliberate how these zealously acquired concepts might affect his classroom behaviour.

The concern in this book is that a significant part of preparation for the profession should be devoted to detection, analysis, development and application of the skills required in teaching, a task complicated by the absence of any clear general agreement as to what these are, as will be seen in Chapters 2, 3 and 4.

There are several strategies under consideration, and the ideas in the book are the result of a wide variety of influences, not the least of which are studies of classroom behaviour, psycho-drama and advances in educational technology.

The teacher's day

Chapters 2 and 3 will describe a number of studies based on live observation of teachers and children in classrooms. By analysing what teachers do when they interact with the children they teach, it is possible to show what the job of teaching may entail. For example, it is clear that teachers ask questions and give information, and that children talk to teachers and to each other, and work singly, in pairs, or in groups. More is being discovered about the nature of these interactions.

Large-scale surveys in primary school classrooms by Duthie[2] in Scotland and Hilsum and Cane[3] in England have provided a great deal of useful information about the teacher's day. In the Hilsum and Cane study 129 teachers in sixty-six different schools were under observation:

> Analysis of the activities that made up the junior teacher's complete working day demonstrated that only 26 per cent of the day was spent actually instructing pupils; about 40 per cent was occupied in the essential related work – organizing pupils (10 per cent), consultation (12 per cent), marking (10 per cent), lesson planning and professional reading (8 per cent). Nearly 25 per cent of the day was spent on clerical and mechanical chores and supervision; almost as much time as was spent instructing.[4]

There were naturally many variations around these means, but in essence the variety of managerial, clerical, instructional and pastoral skills needed to function effectively is quite considerable. For this reason the simulation techniques described in Chapter 5 are sometimes used to explore planning and organisation problems, for to be able to operate well in these areas is a more than useful weapon in the teacher's armoury.

Teaching skills

How can one improve the novice's 'skill' in teaching when there are few if any commonly agreed criteria of effectiveness? The literature dealing with criteria, as will be shown below, is rife with contradictions. As quickly as one researcher finds that his sample of 'good' teachers make extensive use of praise, another finds they do not. No sooner are warmth, extraversion or sensitivity identified as critical personality qualities of the competent teacher, than someone else finds a sample where they are not significantly associated with teaching skill. Even the means for identifying skills are varied. Some use headmasters' reports, others gains on test scores, yet others pupils' ratings or self-assessment procedures.

What has failed significantly is the quest for the philosopher's stone, the omni-purpose 'good teacher' stereotype, the mould into which all newcomers can be poured, Chapter 1 will show how the confidence of earlier generations has given way to a general twentieth-century doubt and lack of certainty. Whereas the classical Chinese teacher could find firm guidelines in the *Book of Rites*, the sixteenth-century Jesuit teacher/priest could follow the *Ratio Studiorum*, and Lancaster's boy monitors would learn in a matter of hours how to teach mechanically to their mentor's formula, the twentieth-century teacher trainee is beset by uncertainties. If a wide range of practices is to be considered acceptable, though this will depend very much on the particular country concerned, what is the meaning of words and concepts such as 'competence' and 'professional standards'?

There are two answers, I think. First of all the focus on competence must be reduced from macro- to micro-scale. In other words the search for a multi-purpose skills kit must be abandoned. More to the point is what are judged to be the needs of a trainee or a group of trainees in particular circumstances. Take, for example, a timid but well intentioned eighteen-year-old girl, hoping to teach nursery or infant; a thirty-five-year-old ex-serviceman, who is a mature entrant to the profession, heading for junior school; and a twenty-two-year-old physics graduate who hopes that teaching will enable him to 'carry on with his physics'. All three, in one sense, are trainee teachers, yet the combination, among other factors, of personal qualities, prior experience, academic background and age makes each unique. Any presupposition that good teachers must leap around the room always smiling (or never smiling for that matter) is going to make some recruits feel miserably inadequate. Good teaching can only be assessed in context. If the purpose of a particular teaching/ learning exercise is that children should pass a test or learn a skill, the success of that exercise will be judged by the number of children who are brought up to a certain level. The rest of the world might be horrified, but within the microcosm that is the criterion of success. If, on the other hand, happiness is the goal, then success equals the number of happy people produced. Most schools, however, hope for neither extreme from their children, but rather a diffuse and often ill defined combination of skills and knowledge to be acquired and personal characteristics to be developed. The teacher's skill is then judged by his ability to produce results in both areas.

The second answer is that since teachers, apart from their pre-service and in-service training periods, are largely responsible for setting their own professional standards, they can most profitably acquire the technique of rigorous self-appraisal at an early stage. Much of what is described in this book will put the trainee in a position where he has to explore various styles of teaching and organisation, and filter several sources of feedback to elicit his own answers. The judgements of experienced observers, be they teachers, tutors or inspectors of various kinds, will comprise one important source of feedback, which some students may judge to outweigh all others, but the student's own per-ceptions, including his readings of children's responses, are of central importance in any behaviour change. Ultimately the teacher must want to change in the light of what he perceives. Only then will significant changes take place.

This may sound gloomy. A former colleague could never understand all the debates about reform in teacher training. He would say, 'I know how to teach and I shall tell them.' In his own way he was effective, but I would rather put it like this: 'I have some experience of both teaching children and preparing students for the profession. I am prepared to use this as needed, and, though not with certainty, offer advice and suggestions, vigorously on some occasions. But in the long term I shall try to provide students with many sources of information about their classroom behaviour, and urge them to look for their own clues and tailor their own style of teaching.' The ideas in the book, therefore, are not intended as a blueprint. There are endless possibilities within teacher training, though fashions are in some respects cyclical. There is also constant novelty, and that is what is appealing. A course based exclusively on procedures described in this book would be barren indeed, and it is part of my task to urge that variety and inventiveness should be dynamic elements in any training programme.

Teacher education and training

I have tried to avoid becoming enmeshed in a debate about education versus training, for I do not see them as opposites. Some of the activities in the book come under the heading of training, which is the learning of a particular skill thought to be of use. Others involve a much wider contemplation of issues provoked by acts of behaviour experienced by participants, which some would call education.

If variety is to be an important element of a course for teachers, it is not the purpose of this book to restrict initiative. My support of Flanders' strictures at the beginning of this section was not an argument against the so-called 'theory' of education, for the rigorous study of education can be a very important aspect of a training course. What is of little value, however, is the divorce of *all* such study from practical experience.

Theory and practice can be linked in a number of ways, as will be discussed more fully below. At Exeter we developed a course called 'Teachers, Schools and Children', in which issues such as learning difficulties, social factors influencing school performance, school organisation and the study of groups were raised via videotapes made in the same comprehensive school. Seven children were seen regularly on tapes. They did reading tests, talked about themselves, performed physical skills, and were shown at work and at play. Much of what might be lectured about could be detected by students watching the videotapes and later visiting the school and meeting the teachers and children.

A phenomenological approach allows discussion to begin with events and acts of behaviour and to draw on such bodies of knowledge as exist in books and the experience of participants. It does not prevent systematic study of other issues which might not emerge so naturally. The events can be seen in videotapes, film, or be culled from the experience of live classroom interaction, either in school or in college.

Variety also applies to experience with children. The block practice has been criticised, but it remains the nearest natural equivalent to the real job. If anything, a philosophy of both variety and gradualism is adopted in this book, ie allowing students to have early experience with small groups, even individual children, then with larger groups, and finally with full classes. This can take place inside the college or the school, or away from both, and be controlled, semi-controlled or relatively free of restriction and supervision. Every student learns differently; some may find that the focused skill sessions of micro-teaching offer just the right degree of structure, feedback and supervision, though others may find it repugnant.

Endnote

Most of what is described in the following chapters is written in terms of 'students' and 'colleges'. These generic terms are used to cover more than just novices in colleges of education. For 'student' one should understand any teacher undergoing training, whether before or during his professional career, as most of the techniques can be adapted to suit the professional experiences of those involved. Similarly, 'college' equals college of education, university or any institution responsible for training teachers, and 'tutor' is the person responsible for the programme or supervision, be he college or university tutor, local authority or Department of Education and Science inspector, professional tutor or experienced teacher supervising one student. It is no slight to the sex not mentioned if a tutor or student is subsequently referred to as 'he' or 'she'. There is no case when it might not be either sex, though the infants' school trainee, for example, is much more likely to be a woman in many countries at the present time, and the physics graduate training for secondary schools probably a man.

For notes to Preface see p. 195.

1 Some Historical Exemplars

FACTORS INFLUENCING THE COURSE OF TEACHER EDUCATION AND TRAINING

The history of teacher education runs closely parallel to the history of schools and indeed to that of the society concerned. In modern Communist China the preparation of teachers, with emphasis on service to the people, factory experience for the student teacher and the thoughts of Chairman Mao Tse-tung as its inspiration, bears but slight resemblance to the senseless chanting of the Chinese classics to which generations of trainees had been subjected. Similarly, the issues facing those whose task it is to prepare teachers in contemporary Britain or the United States, where, for the first time, prospects of teacher surplus are in view, are quite different from those which Bell and Lancaster encountered in early nineteenth-century Britain, or Horace Mann in Massachusetts in 1840, when qualified teachers were scarce and the demand for popular education was beginning to grow.

There are several factors which can determine the content and pattern of teacher education programmes. The sheer size of a country can produce proportionate difficulties, as in China in 1956, for example, when the Ministry of Education estimated that over one million new teachers would be needed in the following seven years. The problem of size is sometimes compounded by the after-effects of war, so that in the late 1940s the USSR had to face rebuilding its institutions without the aid of its 20 million dead of World War II. In Japan also one in four houses had been destroyed and some cities in both Japan and Germany were almost completely obliterated.

Some postwar priorities are clear, such as the need for denazification of German teacher training in the period from 1945 onwards. Occasionally wars produce a welcome bonus, though the price paid has usually been a heavy one. In both the United States and Britain emergency training programmes after both world wars, despite the need for expediency, relative brevity of courses and many large classes, produced new ideas and procedures which persisted long after the courses had ceased to exist. In addition the arrival of large numbers of mature recruits, often with a high level of skill and experience, tended to alter, substantially in certain cases, the nature of the training institution.

Social conditions of the time have proved powerful determinants in the pattern of teacher preparation. Bell and Lancaster at the beginning of the nineteenth century saw the need to provide teachers for vast numbers of boys and girls of working-class families who spent most of their days labouring in mills and factories or on the land. The requirement of Sir Robert Peel's 1802 Factory Act that they should receive instruction in the three Rs and religion on Sundays was often ignored by the factory and mill owners. The situation was made worse by the dire poverty of the children and the almost total lack of any educational tradition in the families. In this context the monitorial system, which used older children to teach the younger ones, was a brilliant, if in retrospect obvious, solution. The brief mechanical nature of the monitors' training was almost inevitable, since extended and more leisurely education would have seemed a cruel luxury, enjoyed by a minority at the expense of the suffering mass. The privileged few who were able to enjoy a lengthy and broad education at that time tended, with some notable exceptions, to make little contribution to the education and welfare of the working-class population.

Religious organisations have frequently used their autonomy and experience to establish sectarian centres of teacher education or to influence existing institutions and patterns of training. This was notable in countries such as Ireland, India, Germany and the United States, where different religions competed for devotees and needed to some extent to spread into teaching in order to reach people at an early age. It was not solely, however, to compete or to maintain a position of strength that led to the foundation of religiously based training institutions. The tradition of preparing others to teach is often rooted in the very beginnings of a religious movement, and Christ's own recruitment and preparation of disciples has parallels in the history of other great religious and political movements. Mao Tse-tung's early experiences at the strongly humanist First Teachers' Training School at Changsha, and later as a primary school teacher and headmaster, were important to the development of his political thought, and subsequently led him to recruit and inspire others who would teach his political ideas to the nation.

In Europe the Jesuits, especially in the period 1450 to 1850, introduced a systematisation of teacher training which was almost without precedent. Books such as the *Ratio Studiorum*, produced in 1586 and revised in 1599, were blueprints which described teaching techniques in detail and were followed almost to the letter. In Tsarist Russia under Peter the Great, in the late seventeenth and early eighteenth centuries, all available teachers were priests, and most of them had been trained at theological seminaries. When Catherine II established a pedagogical seminary at St Petersburg to reduce the teacher shortage, she was largely dependent on the bishops' willingness to release candidates from the theological seminaries. Since they were understandably reluctant to surrender their best students, they responded by sending some of their more lazy and drunken students.

The teacher-priest, nevertheless, tended to be a formidable figure, a man of great breadth and authority. Dean Church describes the role he might play in a rural parish in England.

> When communication was so difficult and infrequent, he filled a place in the country life of England that no one else could fill. He was often the patriarch of his pupils, its ruler, its doctor, its lawyer, its magistrate, as well as its teacher, before whom vice trembled and rebellion dared not show itself.[1]

In Britain the Church was the first body to establish a system of licences for its teachers in the Middle Ages, when it also formed teaching orders. The Church of England in the nineteenth century was instrumental in creating two of the very first training colleges

17

– St Luke's College, Exeter, and the College of St Mark and St John in London. Before this, the fact that Joseph Lancaster was a Quaker significantly influenced the pattern of training received by his monitors.

The religious orders have at various times and in many countries played an important part in the education and training of teachers, but at the same time a vigorous secular tradition has developed, reaching its height at the present day. Universities have figured prominently in these developments, although they tended to have religious connections in the earlier part of their history. In most countries a university degree has entitled its holder to teach, usually at secondary level, but graduates have entered elementary schools, too. No further training was deemed necessary, as is still the case with university teaching itself in the greater part of the world.

One of the most interesting aspects of the secular tradition in teacher education is the style of influence developed by its exponents. With a religious order many of the possible channels of communication and control are already established. There are devotees, buildings, a tradition, a hierarchy, administrative expertise and considerable authority in the community. Pioneers in the secular field have often begun with none of these.

In some cases those who have influenced the course and content of teacher education have been practitioners like Pestalozzi and Froebel, running schools or working with children, and using methods which attracted international attention and led to frequent visits from abroad as well as invitations to assist in the training of new or experienced teachers. Some of the so-called 'great educators', such as Montessori and Dewey, became very active in the training of teachers, whereas others, like A. S. Neill, positively resisted attempts to institutionalise their 'methods' or lure them into moving out of their schools and into teacher training.

Most of the best known and most influential figures had considerable personal dynamism and charisma. Froebel, for example, was very excited after a visit to Yverdon to see Pestalozzi. They fired others with enthusiasm by their example. David Stow, whose

Glasgow Normal Seminary was, in 1837, years ahead of its time in terms of sophistication and methodological variety and subtlety, was inundated with visitors, most of whom were very impressed by what they saw, especially when they compared it with the relative sterility of Bell's monitorial training scheme. Fuller[2] describes a tour made by stagecoach in 1840 by the first Principal of St Luke's College, Exeter, and a member of the Exeter Diocesan Board. A contemporary account of their tour and report shows how a visit of this kind can be influential in affecting the content and nature of a training course: 'They were of the opinion that some of the improvements suggested by Mr Stow and others in the practice of teaching may, with propriety, be engrafted on Dr Bell's system, but recommended that the introduction of these should be made with caution.'[3]

A significant factor in the in-service training of teachers has always been the head of the school, especially in the smaller units of the elementary sector. To a large extent the British 'primary school revolution' was pressed through vigorously, often in the face of severe counter-pressures from parents, teachers or authorities, by this hardy and intrepid band of pioneers, many of whom would work in the classrooms with their teachers until the changes were effected.

Seaborne reports a retired primary school teacher recalling vividly the details of her teaching in 1910:

My headmistress was very foreseeing. She was one of the first people to help us to realise that we should stop teaching children in the mass and to see that they were little individuals. We started to teach 'free arithmetic'; we bought rolls of paper and measured them with the children and we began to go to the shops for boxes. We cut pictures out from advertisements and the rooms began to look brighter. The headmistress fought a battle with the HMIs (His Majesty's Inspectors) and local people, and we did no set arithmetic in the infants' department. No doubt the most important mark we made was in the beginning to get children to live with numbers, and enjoy them.[4]

These then are some of the factors which have helped shape the

19

history of teacher education and training: social and political pressures, wars, religious organisations, the great educators, and the zeal of individual practitioners in schools and training institutions.

It is clearly outside the scope of this chapter to give detailed histories of all civilised and primitive societies' attempts to prepare their teachers, but there follows a consideration of a number of the many interesting models reported in the literature.

PRIMITIVE COMMUNITIES

Accounts by anthropologists of twentieth-century primitive communities in New Guinea, Borneo, South America or Africa, or by historians depicting the early stages of industrialised societies like Britain and the United States, abound with descriptions of teaching. It is quite clear that a great deal of teaching takes place in tribes and families. What is missing in most cases, however, is formal training for those who do the teaching. To know something or to possess a skill is to be in a position to teach it to others.

Since there is often common agreement within the tribe about what children need to learn, such as the basic skills of hunting, cooking, making materials and weapons, and perhaps certain tribal dances and rituals, much of the teaching is informal. Indeed in some tribes care of children is a task given to trusted tribe members quite early in their lives. Okafor-Omali describes the practice in Nigeria:

> Nweke was only four months old when his mother entrusted him completely to the care of a baby-nurse. Baby-nurses were generally children of about eight to ten years. It was their duty to take care of the child and keep him playing while the mother was busy in the compound or at the farm or market . . .
> This work was usually done by members of the child's family or extended family, or by a close relation of the mother with good personal qualifications. It was a matter of pride for children to have such an assignment and they were happy to be relieved, to some extent, from domestic work.[5]

Subsequently all children tend to be the responsibility of their

20

mothers for the early part of their lives, after which boys become attached to their fathers and girls to other women in the tribe as well as their own mother.

Where parents or close relatives do not have a high level of performance in a skill thought to be important for the children, there is often a competent and respected member of the tribe who is willing or even expected to teach it. He is 'untrained' and 'unqualified' in any formal sense, yet, because of the intimacy of the society in which he lives, common acknowledgement of his skill and ability to teach it are clearly sufficient. Were he manifestly unskilled or unable to teach children, he would be unlikely to attract pupils, especially where some token payment is made.

Smith gives what is probably a fairly accurate, if slightly idealised, version of the primitive system at its best:

> In the earlier order of things the father educated his son by a varied life out of doors, by growing food and breeding cattle, and the boy acquired his skill at an early age. His object lessons were got from the smithy, the weaver's shed, the mill, and the carpenter's shop, and his imagination was fired by the stories and legends which belonged to the familiar woods and streams and the neighbouring castle and manor.[6]

At its worst the primitive system produced teachers who were charlatans; they extorted money from their more simple and trusting fellows, and were cruel, perhaps even expected to be cruel, to the children in their care, and education and training based on nothing but each individual's perception of how children learn produced sterotyped and ineffective teaching.

In certain respects the primitive model has persisted well into modern times. The self-appointed local teacher, often barely ahead of his pupils in the skills he was teaching, was widely known in Britain in the mid-nineteenth century, as advertisments in shop windows, such as the following from Wellcombe in Devon in 1851, reveal:

> Roger Giles, Surgin, Parish Clark and Skulemaster, Groser, and Hundertaker, Respectably informs ladys and gentlemen that he

drors teef without wateing a minit, applies laches every hour, blisters on the lowest terms, and vizieks for a penny a peace. He sells Godfather's Kordales, kuts korns, bunyons, doktors hosses, clip donkies, wance a munth, and undertakes to luke arter every bodies nayles by the ear. Joes-harps, penny wissels, brass kannel-sticks, fryinpans, and other moozikal Hinstrumints hat grately reydooced figers. Young ladys and genelmen larnes their grammur and langeudge, in the purtiest manner, also grate care is taken off their morrels and spellin. Also zarm-zinging, tayching the base vial, and all other zarts of vancy work, squadrils, pokers, weazils, and all country dances tort at home and abroad at perfekshun. Perfumery and Znuff, in all its branches. As times is cruel bad, I begs to tell ey that i his just beginned to sell all sorts of stashonery ware, cox, hens, vouls, pigs, and all other kinds of poultry . . . P.S. I tayches gography, rithmetic, cowsticks, jimnastiks, and other chynees tricks.[7]

Despite his Renaissance Man self-image poor Roger Giles was obviously down on his luck, but he deserves some credit for both persistence and divergent thinking.

CLASSICAL MODELS

Although features of the primitive system of self-elected or communally approved teachers without formal qualifications and training, whose pupils used them as their models, have survived into modern times, in the so-called 'classical' periods of Greece and Rome, and earlier still in China and India, teachers received more systematic preparation for their profession.

The nature of professional training has been contingent upon firstly what was deemed to be important for children to learn in a particular society, and secondly upon the philosophy of the person entrusted with the task of preparing the teachers. Broudy has drawn attention to three elements in the first of these:

In every age the school has been expected to provide, first of all *linguistic skills*, the basic tool of learning in any well-developed culture. It is most surprising, therefore, that much of the history of pedagogy hovers about the ways and means of teaching language – for the most part, Latin and Greek as foreign languages. Next in the order of expectation was *a stock of knowledge* – whatever knowledge was in vogue: what the poets said, or what the astronomers, astrologers, theologians, physicists, and alchemists certified as truth. Finally, it was expected that instruction would build into the pupil *habits* of using his acquired skill and knowledge in the forum or in the courts of law and kings, as teachers and prelates, princes and ambassadors, doctors, clergymen, lawyers, scientists, and statesmen, or, in later centuries, as tradesmen, workers, and citizens.[8]

In ancient India knowledge of the sacred texts was held to be of great importance. The teacher had to be very familiar with the content and meaning of the scriptures. Essentials of his training to teach others were self-knowledge and humility. To achieve all these objectives he was attached to the household of his own teacher or guru for quite a lengthy period of time. His task was to serve the guru in however menial a way, to acquire from him wisdom, a way of living and ultimately the supreme goal of knowledge of Brahman, the Absolute.

The Bible contains similar teacher-priest models both in the Old Testament and the New, where Christ's preparation of his own disciples illustrates this pattern of training. They, too, had to share his way of life and learn from his insights before being sent out to teach others.

Holmes highlights the special importance of the teacher of teachers at this time: 'If, however, the teacher is one of a professional group charged with special tasks, what should be his training? An ancient tradition places great stress on the need for close personal contact with a practising teacher and on the desirability of learning through long and supervised experience.'[9]

Confucius, himself a successful teacher at the age of twenty, resigned his post as Chief Justice in China in the fifth century BC to wander around with his disciples. They, too, lived and worked with him before being released to go their own way as teachers. In the Chinese tradition his views on teaching were also set down in written form to be studied by future disciples. His philosophy of teaching, as set down in the *Analects*, is full of shrewd observation, much of which would not be out of place in modern texts:

> I shall not teach until the pupils desire to know something, and I do not help unless the pupils really need my help. If out of the four corners of a subject I have dealt thoroughly with one corner and the pupils cannot then find out the other three for themselves, then I do not explain any more. (*Analects* VII, 8)[10]

The authoritative book on teaching methods is found at various stages of history in ancient China. It is at the heart of any new developments during the various dynasties, and familiarity with it was a prerequisite for the trainee teacher. Richardson describes the stereotyped teaching to which it could lead:

> It is explained in the classic Book of Rites (Li Chi) how the training is to be accomplished: the moral by word of mouth and the practical or technical by imitation and emulation of the teacher. The teacher reads out the principles and the pupils repeat them after him, echoing every intonation and stress, and this is continued until the pupils are word-perfect. The teacher performs the action in the ceremony or dance or musical or military exercise and the pupils slavishly follow his every movement, and this is repeated until the pupils are action perfect.[11]

The Chinese pattern of the teacher as the paragon ideal, the model on which learners were to base their development, has survived to the present day, as has the chanting of the mentor's wisdom. The *Sab Zi Jing* (*Three Character Classic*), written in 960 AD, was still being taught by peasants to their sons as late as the 1950s. Once the classic had been long extant, the children understood little of what they were repeating, but teachers were not being trained to question the mindlessness of the activity, so it survived. Wu Yun-duo describes the hostility which might greet any deviation from the pattern: 'The master never explained anything, and when I asked a question, he simply stared me into silence.'[12]

In contrast to the Chinese experience, trainee teachers in

classical Greece and Rome were often exposed to a variety of patterns, some of which could be quite disturbing in their lack of an authoritarian lead. The early stages of teaching in Athens merely exposed children to good examples from parents and other respected members of the community. Subsequently they would meet teachers who would develop whatever skills were thought to be important at the time. Isocrates, for example, developed the model of the rhetoric teacher. To hold his own a young man of democratic Athens would need to be able to argue a point of view or stand up in public and make a speech. His teachers, therefore, would need to be skilled rhetoricians themselves, and much of the teaching, though it tended at its worst to become systematised imitation, was designed to make pupils verbally alert. Protagoras was so well esteemed as a teacher of oratory and skill in argument that he was able to charge 10,000 drachmas from parents who wished their sons to be turned into successful men of affairs in three or four years.

For Socrates the final stage of education was liberation, the very element missing from much of classical Chinese teaching. The pupil was liberated when his questioning led him to reject habit and prejudice.

> No-one can teach, if by teaching we mean the transmission of knowledge, in any mechanical fashion from one person to another. The most that can be done is that one person who is more knowledgeable than another can, by asking a series of questions, stimulate the other to think, and so cause him to learn for himself.[13]

None of the well known Greek and Roman teachers was solely a teacher of teachers. Of course, many of their pupils did themselves become teachers, and sitting at the feet of a distinguished man was at least a considerable boost to prestige even if not a prerequisite.

The Sophists, like Protagoras, Prodicus of Ceos and Giorgias of Leontini, subjected known examples of good writing to systematic analysis, and this led to the creation of what were virtually teaching handbooks by later figures such as Dionysius of Thrace, who laid down a sequence of steps to be followed when giving a lecture on a literary work (166 BC):

1 Give the selected passages an exact reading with respect to pronunciation, punctuation, and rhetorical expression.
2 Explain the figures of speech.
3 Explain the historical and mythological references.
4 Comment on the choice of words and their etymology.
5 Point out the grammatical forms employed.
6 Estimate the literary merit of the selection.[14]

In Rome Cicero and Quintilian analysed teaching methodology in considerable detail, and their analysis of, for example, delivering a lecture on a topic, or asking children to write sentences which copied the style of the writer being studied, were extremely influential.

The teacher-orator model is seen in Christian times later on. St Augustine, who educated Christian teachers, emphasised that knowledge of the scripture was not sufficient. Trainees had to be trained in the skills of oral expression so they could both communicate meaning to their pupils and, if necessary, defend their faith against the educated non-believer in public.

In later times when classical ideals were revived, Cicero's techniques were still held in esteem. The twelfth-century scholar Peter Abelard, who also taught teachers, made extensive use of discussion and debate in his own teaching. Eventually skill in argument was judged and became a prerequisite for early teaching licences. Students at medieval universities who could demonstrate their skill might be accepted as members of a teachers' guild. At the University of Paris in the thirteenth century students were trained in the skills of lecturing and were then asked to dispute a thesis with a master before a board of examiners. If successful, they would be granted the chancellor's licence to teach. At Bologna University a candidate for a bachelor's degree had to have given a course of lectures to other students in order to get his degree. The poorer performers had to bribe their fellows to get an audience.

Alongside the trained rhetoric teacher in classical Rome was a strong father-teacher image. Horace, in his *Satires*, describes his father as 'always present, an incorruptible overseer, at all my studies'.[15] As in earlier societies, a boy might later be handed over to a personal tutor at about the age of sixteen. This man would usually have experience and good reputation, and often be held in much greater esteem than the Greek or Roman elementary schoolmaster, who was not highly regarded. Lucian classed elementary schoolmasters with sellers of kippers in terms of poverty, and they had a reputation for administering cruel corporal punishment. The personal tutor would initiate the boy into public life. Cicero himself was attached to Quintus Mucius Scaevola, a distinguished lawyer.

The features of teacher training in classical societies which distinguish it from primitive cultures are that some of the methodology was written in books for students to learn; that attachment to a distinguished scholar, orator, philosopher or religious leader was sufficient to qualify a person to teach what he had learned, provided he had also absorbed the required way of life; that teaching methods were being systematically analysed and some attention was being given to how children learned; and that in certain cases both teaching and preparation for teaching were becoming stereotyped and unrelated to the needs of the students. Seneca, in his *Epistles*, voices a common lament: 'Non vitae sed scholae discimus' ('We learn not for life but for school').[16]

TEACHER TRAINING IN INDUSTRIALISED SOCIETIES

The advent of large-scale industralisation in many European countries in the late eighteenth and early nineteenth centuries produced a concomitant increase in the size of cities. In addition, pressure was being applied for compulsory education for children, and the lack of sufficient 'qualified' teachers was clearly an obstacle to progress.

Consequently much of the experience in all countries at the early stages of their industrial evolution centres around expediency. The pressing need was to produce as many respectable candidates for teaching as possible, rapidly cement the more gaping holes in their own education, and process them through a brief teaching methods programme whose emphasis was on survival skills. It was merely one further exercise in mass production to match the methods seen to be effective in the factories.

There were few other models on which to base training programmes. The primitive and classical patterns described above were known, of course, but they tended to presuppose small numbers of highly motivated and often privileged pupils. Occasionally one country, such as Prussia, would be ahead in some respect, but its experience might not be of value to others at a more rudimentary stage. Rich describes the situation in the early days of the training colleges:

England was far behind her Continental neighbours in the establishment of training colleges, and her earliest efforts were almost uninfluenced by what was taking place abroad. The result was that whilst on the Continent they were busy instructing their teachers, rather than showing them how to teach, in England the main emphasis was laid on the actual methods of instructions.[17]

Much of the teacher training before the Industrial Revolution had in any case been done by the Church or the universities. The universities had concentrated to a large extent on subject matter, and, with very few exceptions, had ignored preparation in teaching methods. Some of the teaching orders, notably the Jesuits, had analysed teaching strategies in considerable detail, but their special emphasis on character training, while influential, was not central to the needs of an illiterate mass. Nevertheless the Jesuit style of teacher training was one of the most highly organised and documented. Each pupil was to be matched with another member of the class whose task it was to expose his mistakes. Competition was emphasised, small teams of two or three pupils being matched against others during the year. Teachers were urged to make extensive use of praise, to refrain from sarcasm, not to have favourites, not to speak to pupils outside class, and to review the week's material every Saturday. Books like the *Ratio Studiorum* (1586) detailed teaching methods with considerable thoroughness and attention to detail:

> If an oration or poem is being explained, first its meaning must be explained, if it is obscure, and the various interpretations considered. Second, the whole method of the workmanship, whether invention, disposition, or delivery is to be considered, also how aptly the author ingratiates himself, how appropriately he speaks, or from what topics he takes his material for persuading, for ornament, or for moving his audience; how many precepts he unites in one and the same place, by what method he includes with the figures of thought the means of instilling belief, and again the figures of thought which he weaves into the figures of words. Third, some passages similar in subject matter and expression are to be adduced and other orators or poets who have used the same precept for the sake of proving or narrating something similar are to be cited. Fourth, let the facts be confirmed by statements of authorities, if opportunity offers. Fifth, let statements from history, from mythology, and from all erudition be sought which illustrate the passage. At last, let the words be considered carefully, and their fitness, their elegance, their number, and their rhythm noted. However, let these things be considered, not that the master may always discuss everything, but that from them he may select those which are most fitting.[18]

While of great importance to the teaching orders, such wisdom clearly had little relevance to the preparation of boy monitors for teaching illiterate pupils who had found themselves, sometimes reluctantly, and usually with no family tradition of schooling, in the monitorial schools of the early nineteenth century.

Bell and Lancaster

At the beginning of the nineteenth century in Britain there were already a number of 'schools' in existence. Many working-class children in towns would only attend a Sunday school, such as the one founded by John Wesley in 1737, where the emphasis was on Biblical knowledge and reading. In the villages children from rural backgrounds might attend one of the numerous dame schools run

29

by a wide variety of usually elderly ladies who charged a small fee in return for giving elementary instruction in reading and numbers. The dames were almost inevitably untrained, and on their death or retirement the schools might disappear altogether, or else the 'franchise' might be passed on to a trusted neighbour.

The Society for Promoting Christian Knowledge (SPCK) ran a number of charity schools from the end of the seventeenth century. A notable feature of these schools was that they used pupil-teachers, and furthermore that they attempted to train them in an elementary way by sending them to watch experienced teachers at work (to London schools, if necessary) or by attaching them to an older colleague in a local school for supervised practice.

Alongside these were the schools for older children, the private or common day schools. The men who ran these had no formal training and were often poorly educated themselves. They often had formidable reputations for drunkenness and cruelty to the children in their care. It was partly out of revulsion for these wretches, described by Joseph Lancaster as 'too often the refuse of superior schools, and of society at large', that he and Andrew Bell set up the monitorial system.

Dr Andrew Bell had been an army captain in Madras, where he had encouraged older children to stay on at school to teach the beginners. In 1797 he published a pamphlet describing the methods he had used, and in 1798 and 1799 applied his system to schools in Aldgate and Kendal. Meanwhile, in 1798, Joseph Lancaster, a twenty-year-old Quaker, started the Borough Road School. It was not unusual at that time for very young people to have charge of schools containing as many as 400 children. To Bell's chagrin, Lancaster, on reading the pamphlet, began to apply a great deal of energy to improving and augmenting the Madras method, and the succeeding long arguments about who invented the monitorial system became even more bitter when Lancaster gained the approval of George III and international recognition.

'What Lancaster did was to apply the method on such a scale and to organise it in so complete a fashion that the problem of numbers in a school seemed to be solved, and the question of cost abolished.'[19] Lancaster in his 1810 book *The British System of*

Education explained his training system in detail. The school was divided into eight classes as follows:

Class 1	ABC
Class 2	Words of syllables of 2 letters
Class 3	Words of syllables of 3 letters
Class 4	Words of syllables of 4 letters
Class 5	Words of syllables of 5 letters
Class 6	Reading or spelling lessons of 2 syllables and New Testament
Class 7	Bible study
Class 8	A selection of the best readers from Class 7

The teacher would choose the best pupils in the school to act as monitors, as Lancaster argued that any pupil who could read could teach others to read. Some of the material the monitors had to teach, however, was so baffling in its complexity that few of them understood it themselves. Reading Sheet number 14 for the seventh class of the Northampton Lancasterian School contains passages such as: 'If thy brother be waxen poor, and fallen in decay with thee; then thou shalt relieve him; yea, though he be a stranger or a sojourner; take thou no usury of him, or increase.'[20]

By 1820 about 200,000 children were being taught in over 1,500 Bell or Lancaster monitorial schools. Lancaster was urging the general public 'to consider no person practically qualified to teach (on the "British" plan) who have not a certificate from J. Lancaster of their having been under his care.'[21]

Both Bell and Lancaster aimed at austerity and efficiency. Training was limited (Bell claimed he only needed 24 hours), and the monitors spent most of their time actually teaching, and often learning the material themselves in the process. Even such strategies as classroom commands were to be given in stereotyped form. Despite this, Lancaster personally regarded his monitors as a family, and he spent a great deal of his spare time with them. He also gave them a rather primitive 'theory' course which consisted of a series of lectures on the 'passions'. Bell scorned this approach: 'It is by attending the school, seeing what is going on

31

there, and taking a share in the office of tuition, that teachers are to be formed, and not by lectures and abstract instruction.'[22]

His preparation for the monitors was essentially practical:

> The course of training was largely a matter of 'learning by doing'. However, it began with a study of books that explained the system, 'manuals of method' in the narrowest sense of the term. When some mastery of the work had been manifested the pupil was placed either as 'teacher' (ie monitor) or assistant in a class, starting at the bottom of the 'sand class', and working up through the school in a period of six or eight weeks.[23]

Such was the success of the method, especially in Lancaster's case, that its principles were widely adopted by other countries all over the world where similar problems were being faced. Lancaster visited Montreal in 1822, and in addition to Royal approval had the support of a number of prominent politicians. There were even moves to get the system adopted nationally: 'The principles upon which he (Lancaster) proceeds at the Free School in the Borough are upon examination, so obviously founded in utility and economy, that they must prevail, and will finally, I have no doubt, furnish a mode of instruction, not only for this country, but for all the nations advanced in any degree of civilisation.'[24]

There was not, however, total satisfaction with the system. A number of those who on the whole supported Lancaster were aware of some of the shortcomings, and one can detect here the modern beginnings of the as yet uncompleted debate about what teachers need to learn. A subcommittee of the British Society, the society which grew out of the Royal Lancasterian School Society, examined the training methods and decided there were some serious defects. It suggested that student teachers' education should be improved in three areas: they should have 'firstly, a knowledge of English grammar sufficient to qualify them to speak and write their own language with correctness and propriety; secondly, the improvement of their handwriting; thirdly, geography and history, and in addition, when time and other circumstances will admit . . . other useful branches of knowledge.'[25]

Many years later the Cross Commission of 1888 pinpointed the flaws in the monitorial system with devasting accuracy:

> They were not even to use a book. Teaching by books was prohibited, at least in the beginning. All they could do was faithfully to transmit the letter of the lesson they had received, for how should they have seized its spirit? Consequently all they were called upon to do was to apply exactly the mechanical processes in which they had been drilled.
> These children under this mechanical discipline often mistook and confounded the formulas they were called upon to apply. The only remedy for this was to drive into them by constant repetition the daily course of instruction.[26]

Despite these valid criticisms, it should be remembered that, given the state of education existing at the time in Britain and other countries which used the monitorial method, many more children received a basic schooling than might have been the case without the boy monitors.

David Stow and the Glasgow Normal Seminary

The founding of the Glasgow Normal Seminary in 1837 was like a breath of fresh air. It placed Scotland well ahead of the rest of Britain in teacher training methods, and several of Stow's former pupils took important positions in schools and teacher training institutions all over the world. In addition, it began a tradition whereby innovations in teacher training spread to schools, with the training institutions providing a valuable source of inspiration.

In 1837 the Glasgow Educational Society opened a unique complex of buildings. There were four 'model' schools graded for various age groups and achievement levels and a so-called 'Normal Seminary'. Rich explains the use of the term 'normal' which was applied extensively to teacher training institutions all over Europe and North America:

> ... the use of the term 'normal' in connection with teachers' training is significant of an 'idol' of the training college – the idea

that there exists some norm or type in teaching, and the nearer the teacher comes to that norm the better will his teaching be. It is this conception that explains the popularity of the model school, which was looked upon as the concrete embodiment of the norm so far as the school as an institution was concerned, whilst the teaching of the master of method was to be regarded as the norm in the technique of class teaching.[27]

Altogether there were sixteen classrooms, playgrounds, a library, a museum, and rooms for 1,000 children and 100 students. Tutors taught 'model' lessons and four students in succession gave 15-minute lessons which were observed by half the trainees sitting and observing while the other half were teaching classes elsewhere. Occasionally the student would be required to teach a public criticism lesson, when the observers' benches would be filled with fellow students, the rector of the Seminary, the heads of the model schools, experienced teachers and often Stow himself. Gallery lessons were always followed by criticism sessions, when the other students or experienced teachers passed their judgements on what they had seen.

The playgrounds of the model schools contained an elaborate assembly of outdoor apparatus. There were poles with ropes attached and circular swings. Part of Stow's philosophy demanded that children should be allowed to let off steam, and student teachers had to join in the activities in the playground as well as insert brief spells of physical jerks into their classroom teaching. After the repressive style of teaching of the traditionally cruel Scottish 'dominie', the sheer humanity of Stow's students was a welcome change. Cruickshank describes the real superiority of the method compared with the Bell and Lancaster system. 'The spirit of Stow's work and the method he employed demanded of the trainees, insight, understanding and a degree of sensitivity associated with maturity.'[28]

The thoroughness of Stow's preparation was remarkable. Although his recruits were usually better educated than the boy monitors had been, he was not satisfied with their level of achievement and set about improving it. They had to learn to be school masters and mistresses in the fullest sense of the terms. They constructed timetables, kept registers and school accounts, and learned to read and carry out government regulations. In addition they had to apply Stow's unique philosophy of teaching, partly based on commonsense, partly on whim, but always stressing deep concern for the children in their care. Stow himself described these novelties:

> First, the addition of direct moral training, in conjunction with the branches usually taught, including the requisite platform and apparatus, with the method of using them; – second, a mode of intellectual communication, termed, 'Picturing out in words', conducted by a combination of questions and ellipses, analogy, and familiar illustrations, – the use of simple terms by the teacher, within the range of the pupil's acquirements, – and answers, chiefly simultaneous, but occasionally individual, by which the pupils are normally trained to observe, perceive, reflect, and judge, and thus to draw the lesson for themselves, and to express it to the trainer in such terms as they fully understand – being made to perceive as vividly by the mental eye as they would real objects by the bodily eye.[29]

Much of what Stow advocated would receive general approval even today: the adventure playgrounds are still popular, student teachers are encouraged not to remain aloof but to join in activities with children. Indeed the 15 minute criticism lesson is not unlike micro-teaching without playback facilities or the re-teach cycle. Some of the psychology, though crudely expressed by Stow, is still relevant today if rephrased in the light of what is currently known about children's thinking. Consequently it is not surprising that elements of the Glasgow Normal Seminary were incorporated in their early stages of development in colleges such as Homerton, Westminster and St Luke's, Exeter, and that the best of the Glasgow trainees were eagerly sought all over the world in preference to Bell and Lancaster's robots.

The early training colleges

Jeffreys has described the embarrassing shortage of good

teachers in a number of countries in the first half of the nineteenth century:

> The remarkable thing in the modern history of education is that it took so long for the various countries to realise the importance of teacher-training – to realise, in fact, that schools cannot be better than their teachers. Throughout the first half of the nineteenth century in England the attempts to establish a general system of elementary education were continually hampered by the hopeless inadequacy of the teachers.[30]

Prussia was in a better position than most other European countries, having had normal schools since the early eighteenth century at Halle (1704), Berlin (1748) and Münster (1759) among others. By the middle of the nineteenth century there were 156 well established normal schools in Germany. Visitors were impressed by the strong esprit de corps among the students and by the high level of their academic work compared with other countries.

In France the *école normale* was founded in 1808 to train teachers for the *lycée*. The emphasis in these institutions was on practical matters, and trainees learned to draw up certificates of birth, death and marriage, as well as to prune trees. By the middle of the nineteenth century the *écoles normales* had become centres of liberation and political agitation. Only the national shortage of teachers protected them from firm government action.[31]

In the United States the Lancasterian method had been used since as early as 1806, and ideas were constantly being brought in from Europe by immigrants and travelling teachers or administrators. The tradition of communities establishing their own schools and training and recruiting teachers for them was already a developing one. By 1837, for example, there were 2,000 schools in various parts of Massachusetts, but few were open for more than 20 weeks of the year, and large numbers of children attended for less than half that time. Horace Mann,[32] the humane and far-seeing Secretary to the State Board of Education, was greatly impressed by the Prussian normal schools, and they were one important source of influence on the Lexington Normal School founded in 1839. Mann was also familiar with the home-produced

36

model seminary for teachers established by Samuel Hall in Vermont in 1823, so he had at least two major sources of inspiration. The founding of the Lexington Normal School was an important development in teacher training in the United States. Not unusually, this was due once again to a particularly energetic and imaginative principal, Cyrus Peirce, who himself taught as many as ten different subjects in one term, seventeen in a year, supervised a model school of thirty pupils, acted as demonstration teacher, developed his own teaching ideas and materials, fulfilled the duties of janitor, and still found time to give the student teachers courses on the science and art of teaching the various subjects.[33]

Mann's efforts did not cease here, despite considerable hostility from the Governor of Massachusetts. He went on to found other normal schools, increasing the amount of time student teachers would spend there (it could be as little as a month initially), and set up a number of impressively elaborate in-service workshops where up to 100 teachers might attend refresher courses, further their education, or watch demonstrations of the latest teaching techniques.

In England a similar pattern began to emerge. The models available to Kay-Shuttleworth when he founded the Battersea College in 1840 were the monitorial system and what he had seen in the European normal schools when he had visited them on his travels. Initially thirteen-year-olds were to be taken for a seven year apprenticeship. They were to study English, Art, Music and practical subjects such as land surveying and accountancy. They were given lectures on the theory of teaching similar to what Kay-Shuttleworth had seen in the 'Paedagogik' lectures in Prussian and Swiss normal schools. They had nature walks, as did the Swiss trainees. Later, in 1846, the pupil-teacher system was made a national scheme, and promising thirteen-year-olds were apprenticed to school managers until they were eighteen and able to go to training colleges proper.

Kay-Shuttleworth himself described the course he gave on the theory and art of teaching:

They have treated of the general objects of education, and means of obtaining them. The peculiar aims of elementary education; the structure of school-houses in various parts of Europe; the internal arrangement of the desks, forms, and school apparatus, in reference to different methods of instruction; and the varieties of those methods observed in different countries. The theory of the discipline of schools . . . To these subjects have succeeded lectures in the great leading disputations in the methods of communicating knowledge.[34]

The certification system was borrowed from Holland, and teachers could take a one, two or three year course with corresponding gains in salary. Most of the early colleges established their own 'practising school', and students were required to spend time doing supervised teaching practice under the supervision of the 'normal master', who was often the only qualified teacher in the school. Rule X of the St Luke's College 1855 Prospectus states:

Every student is expected, whenever he may be required, to become a teacher in the Practising School, under the direction of the Normal Master. His success will mainly depend upon the zeal and efficiency which he displays in this department.[35]

The 'normal master' not only taught at the school but went into the college to lecture. Fuller describes a report on the work of such a teacher. 'Mr Barrett gave a "useful and sensible lecture on the construction of timetables" as well as a lesson on Plato at the Practising School which was "a good specimen of teaching where the lads were very dull."'[36]

The student teachers spent three weeks at a time with the normal master in groups of four. They were able to teach three or four lessons a week which were criticised by the normal master, watch him teach, and occasionally run the whole school for a day. The normal master at the St Luke's Practising School in 1849 had to rate the students formally for such qualities as 'energy as a teacher', 'skill in keeping a class attentive and active', and 'whether the instruction as to matter and manner is addressed to the understanding of the children'.[37]

Despite the obvious progress since the monitorial system, there was still no widespread satisfaction with the training and education of teachers. Teaching methods were criticised. Taylor describes the comments of Her Majesty's Inspector Moseley:

In his report on the training School at Battersea, Moseley was not enthusiastic about the oral method that Kay-Shuttleworth had encouraged. If it made teachers, it did not make students, giving neither the habit of self-instruction, nor the taste for it.[38]

There was concern about the effectiveness of the by now widely used gallery criticism lesson:

The Revd. F. Temple . . . commented upon the limitation of the popular 'gallery' lesson, so called because this was the part of the hall used by one student, who gave a lesson of 15 minutes which was criticised by the other students. There was a tendency to stimulate the other students rather than convey information to the children. 'The business of the schoolmaster is not so much to teach as to make children learn.'[39]

Nor was there agreement about what student teachers should learn. Some of the colleges tried to be severely practical. The St Luke's College 1857 examination papers on school management contained questions such as:

1 To what subjects would you apply Collective Instruction? What are the disadvantages of this method?

5 Draw up a form for a 'Summary of Attendance and Payments' for a school, and fill it up for one quarter.[40]

Other colleges had a syllabus which was less useful to schools. Taylor points out that a number of principals of colleges in the middle of the nineteenth century were Oxbridge clerics with little awareness of the social background of children in elementary schools.[41]

The Principal of the College of St Mark and St John in the 1840s, Derwent Coleridge, 'admitted to taking his models, not from the pedagogical seminaries of Switzerland and Germany that Kay-Shuttleworth so much admired, but from the "older educational institutions of (this) country, originally intended, even those of the higher class, with their noble courts, solemn chapels, and serious cloisters, for clerks to the full as humble as those I had to train." '[42]

The Newcastle Commission in 1861 expressed a number of reservations, and was especially critical of the poor practical training and the superficial nature of much of what was covered. The commission's members pressed for better trained adults and were critical of pupil-teachers who showed 'great meagreness of knowledge, crudeness, and mechanical methods of study, arising largely from neglect of their training by their head teachers'.[43]

So the criticisms were of two kinds. There were those who claimed that pupil-teachers especially, and also newly qualified teachers, were badly prepared for teaching and sparsely educated in any general sense, and others who derided the arrogance of the over-educated teacher:

> He and some one hundred and forty schoolmasters had been lately turned at the same time in the same factory, on the same principles, like so many pianoforte legs ... He knew all about the water sheds of all the world (whatever they are) and all the histories of all the peoples and all the names of all the rivers and the mountains, and all the productions, manners, and customs of all the countries, and all their boundaries and bearings on the two and thirty points of the compass. Ah, rather overdone, M'Choakumchild. If he had only learnt a little less, how infinitely better he might have taught much more?[44]

A hundred years of popular education

It would be difficult to do other than briefly mention a small number of the developments in teacher education and training in the 100 years during which most industrialised societies have had compulsory schooling for all children. There are a number of features, however, common to several countries.

First of all there has been a colossal increase in numbers. Many English colleges of education doubled or trebled in size within relatively short periods of time at various stages in their history, followed by perhaps decades of stability. In the year 1958, for example, 18,000 students began training as teachers, whereas by 1968 the number had increased to 46,500.

Secondly, training has tended to lengthen rather than contract. Except for emergency schemes operating after major wars or other civil disasters, few countries now consider less than three years post secondary school as adequate, many demand four or five years, and in countries with open-ended degree courses, such as Germany, it is possible for a secondary teacher to take seven years or longer over his courses, most of which time is consumed by subject work.

A third factor is the influence of the 'great thinkers'. These were people who might not necessarily train teachers themselves, though some did, but whose thoughts and writings reached the teacher trainer and were interpreted by him to the student in training. In addition to the best known such as Pestalozzi stressing the importance of immediacy, the object lesson, simultaneous instruction of the whole class; Froebel emphasising play, motor forms of activity and aesthetic expression; Dewey, whose activity programme radically broke away from the common recitation lesson formula; psychologists and writers on psychology such as Thorndike; Watson and the later behaviourists like Skinner; Max Wertheimer and the Gestalt school; Freud and his followers Melanie Klein and Susan Isaacs; and T. P. Nunn, whose book *Education, Its Data and First Principles* ran to twenty reprints between 1920 and 1945, there were sociologists, anthropologists, ethologists, and shrewd observers of children in classrooms with a persuasive style of writing like A. S. Neill and more recently John Holt. In fact the college lecturer is overwhelmed at the present time by the plethora of material being produced; and his task of filtering and interpreting, formerly straightforward, has become extremely difficult. The days of the 'normal school' or 'normal master' are past. Vast numbers of teaching models are proclaimed, and there is little common agreement about what constitutes effective teaching.

Rugg has described the beginnings of this change as manifested in the United States:

For twenty years – nearly thirty – there was no split in thought and feeling in Teachers' College or in most of the other teacher-education institutions of the country. The reason is clear – the professors all thought alike. There was no real minority. Not until the 1920s did one appear and then it was tiny.[45]

Despite the changes described above, some writers argue that the basic pattern has remained the same. Dent states his criticism of the colleges over-harshly.

What they (the colleges) did not do, even in this period of extensive and intensive change, was to alter the basic pattern of teacher education. Despite all the modernisation and liberalisation that have occurred over the past century and a half, the 1814 pattern has persisted. Nearly everyone says it must be changed. One hopes the change will be for the better.[46]

It is indeed true that one can point to earlier models and then find training institutions which still have them. For example, there are the 1907 Committee of Seventeen recommendations for the training of secondary school teachers in the United States:

II That definite study be given to each of the following subjects, either in separate courses or in such combinations as convenience or necessity demands:

(a) History of Education:
   1 History of general education.
   2 History of secondary education.
(b) Educational Psychology with emphasis in adolescence.
(c) The principles of education, including the study of educational aims, values and processes. Courses in general method are included under this heading.
(d) Special methods in the secondary school subjects that the students expect to teach.
(e) Organisation and management of schools and school systems.
(f) School hygiene.

III That opportunity for observation and practice teaching with secondary pupils be given.[47]

For some training institutions this might be a broadly accurate description of what is done today, yet within this framework many kinds of variations are possible.

There have certainly been cyclical elements in the history of teacher training. Methods die and are rediscovered in modified form by an exultant future generation. The gallery lesson survives but may be televised or viewed through a one-way screen. The normal master may be a teacher tutor or cooperating teacher in the United States. The monitorial system might be termed 'team teaching' or 'study practice'. The model schools remain in the extensively used campus schools in the United States, though in Britain the trend has been to use almost all available schools. But modern versions have the advantage of a considerable reservoir of earlier models on which to draw, and it is an oversimplification to pretend they have no new elements. It is to some of the newer elements that much of the rest of this book is devoted.

For notes to this chapter see pp 195–7.

2 The Student Teacher

Attempts to modify teacher training programmes need to take into consideration what is known about student teachers, their attitudes, anxieties, motives, personality traits, and, most importantly, their classroom behaviour. Consequently this chapter will attempt to describe some of the studies of student teachers, mainly British ones, and assess their implications for teacher training.

Previous summaries of research by Evans (1961)[1] Allen (1963),[2] Cane (1968),[3] Taylor (1969)[4] and Cope (1970)[5] have indicated just over 100 references. Cane has pointed out the paucity of research generally in this area:

> The salary bill for teachers in maintained schools was £450,000,000 in 1963–64 – nearly half the total L.E.A. and Ministry educational expenditure. This considerable annual investment in some 300,000 teachers on the staff of maintained schools is backed by astonishingly little information about teacher education, and by few research projects which might be of assistance to those concerned with educating teachers.[6]

Taylor, in one of the more thorough reviews of recent research, commented on the lack of studies of the work of the training institutions:

> Until very recently few people have shown much interest in the activities of the Colleges and Departments of Education, and even today much of the best work in the field is on questions of numbers and supply; with very few exceptions, the rest of the available research does not amount to much, and its impact seems to have been negligible.[7]

It is not easy to divide the research into conceptually distinct areas, as some studies have considered several aspects of student teachers' background, personality or training. This review, however, is divided into four sections, largely on the basis of the students' chronological progress through their course. It begins with a consideration of students' backgrounds, motives for choosing teaching as a career and selection procedures. There follows a section on students' attitudes and personality. Thirdly, teaching practice and some of the relevant research into teaching effectiveness are considered. Finally there is a description of some of the follow-up studies which have attempted to trace former students and report on their careers, factors influencing their success or failure, and the effectiveness of their training.

A neat division along these lines is impossible, since many studies overlap several, or even all, of these groups. Nor is it always possible to separate out research into graduate students from research into non-graduates, for many pieces of research include a large or small graduate sample. Obviously there are differences, sometimes significant, between graduate and non-graduate teacher trainees. The University of Toledo (1965)[8] cross-cultural comparison of British and American teacher trainees found the British achievement scores in a number of subject areas very powerfully boosted by the high performance of English and Scottish graduate students. Evans (1964)[9] specifically compared 144 graduates and 145 college students preparing for teaching in the same year on tests of reasoning and personality, and found that the graduates scored significantly higher in reasoning ability as measured by Valentine Reasoning Tests, the AH5 Test of High-grade Intelligence and other tests (although 20 per cent of the college students scored on or above the graduate mean scores), but college students were shown to be significantly more extravert than the graduates on personality tests.

In addition to such research findings where graduate and non-graduate teachers are compared directly, there are two further complications. First of all there is an overlap between institutions. There are graduates undergoing a one year course in colleges alongside college students, and there are graduate courses leading

45

to the BEd degree within the colleges themselves, so that separating out scores between graduates and non-graduates is not easy. Secondly, college students span a greater age-range and could be as young as 18. Most studies of colleges, however, have taken a spread of students over the whole 2, 3 or 4 years of the course to try to overcome the bias which might result from looking only at the youngest group.

One other point which will be made both now and in the course of the review is that the studies which have been made are of uneven quality. Some are interesting but out of date, others are modern but based on a poor or unrepresentative sample. There are studies which are well carried out on a good sample and carefully reported, studies which report findings and give guidelines about future practices about which many readers would express grave doubts, and studies which provide data supported by no other investigation. Nevertheless much of the research available is being reviewed, and such qualifications, reservations or critical analyses which need to be expressed will be given in the context of the piece of research described.

STUDENTS' BACKGROUND, MOTIVES FOR WANTING TO TEACH, SELECTION PROCEDURES

The social background of student teachers has been the subject of a number of studies. Floud and Scott (1961),[10] in a substantial enquiry, showed that the social origins of teachers in various kinds of schools were significantly different. There was a higher percentage of recruits from working-class families in primary and secondary modern schools than there was in grammar and direct grant schools. It was further shown that in all types of schools women tended to be of higher social origin than men.

The Robbins Report (1964)[11] included an analysis of the social background of students in both universities and colleges of education which also showed that a higher percentage of students from working-class homes attended colleges than universities.

Two more recent studies tend to confirm some of the patterns noted in the earlier research. Ashley, Cohen and Slatter (1967)[12] studied samples of graduate and non-graduate trainee teachers. Analysis of fathers' occupations showed that 21 per cent of male graduate teacher trainees and only 8 per cent of female had fathers from the Registrar General's social classes 4 and 5. The corresponding figure for college of education students was 45 per cent of men and 35 per cent of women.

Isaac (1969)[13] found that in one North of England college 62 per cent of a sample of 266 students had fathers who had not attended grammar school, and 57 per cent fathers belonging to the Registrar General's classes 3, 4 and 5. Only 4 per cent of fathers were in social class 1. As reported by Isaac, his conclusion that there is need for greater emphasis on group discussions in colleges because of the strong working-class element is more of an interesting suggestion than a research finding.

In the United States Wright and Tuska (1966)[14] made a comparison between student teachers and other students of similar age and background, and found that the student teachers were more likely to recollect unsatisfactory relationships with their fathers than the others, more likely to recall the influence of a particular teacher, and more likely to feel greater admiration for that teacher than they felt for their own mother. The researchers' conclusion was that the identification with teachers by children was likely to be a considerable influence on their eventual choice of teaching as a career. This is an American study which it would be interesting to replicate in Britain.

Altman (1967)[15] investigated the motives of mature student teachers for leaving other occupations and taking up teaching, and found that usually they were reasonably successful and satisfied with middle-class or lower-middle-class jobs, even though many were from working-class backgrounds. Few of them would be earning a better salary in teaching, yet they were attracted to a job which, they felt, offered opportunities to be creative and original. They rated 'opportunity to be helpful to others' first on a list of ten alternatives and 'attractive salary' very much lower.

Motives for entering the teaching profession have been investigated by a number of researchers since as early as 1934.

Clearly, as social conditions change, so too will expressed motives for entering teaching.

Probably the earliest enquiry into the motives of graduates entering the teaching profession was undertaken by Valentine (1934).[16] His sample of 195 men and 153 women gave 'economic desirability' (men) and 'love of subject' (women) as first choice. An important factor at that time was the availability of a grant, and this came as second choice for men, for whom economic desirability and availability of a grant clearly outweighed the 'love of children/love of subject' motive more readily expressed in affluent times. Another factor high on the list of both men and women in the Valentine enquiry is 'parental wish', a choice which has disappeared in later enquiries and is another indicator of social changes in the last 40 years.

By the time Tudhope (1944)[17] conducted his enquiry among training college students, the war was nearly over and the depression would be a childhood memory of his sample. 'Job security' and 'love of children' were given as the first two reasons by his sample of 216 men and 427 women. Men put 'job security' first and women chose 'love of children'. Among the women, 'earning a good salary' came third or fourth on the list, and junior/secondary trainees ranked 'love of subject' higher than junior/infant students.

The present writer[18] investigated a group of ninety postgraduate students and found that the two most popular motives given were 'love of children' and 'love of subject'. Salary, parental wish and security were barely mentioned.

Veness (1962)[19] went one stage further back and asked school-leavers which jobs appealed to them, and those indicating an interest in teaching tended to stress the helping influencing aspect. Many wrote of their fondness for children or of a desire to work with children and teach them things they (the school-leavers) knew, but very few mentioned the security aspect of the job. Problems of discipline were cited as unattractive features of teaching, and even of those who said teaching was a job they would like to do, few described it as their ideal job.

Some students came to their training with teaching experience behind them. Such experience has not been shown to confer lasting or significant advantages on those who have experienced it: Pinsent (1933)[20] found it had little effect on the theory marks of graduates, as did Turnbull (1934),[21] who did, however, find it gave a small advantage in practical teaching. Saer (1941)[22] also found that graduates with prior teaching experience did no better than those who had none. Since all this research is now out of date, the time is probably ripe for further analysis of the influence of previous experience on the teaching performance of student teachers. In the past people coming into teacher training with previous experience were perhaps likely to be those who had tried teaching and found difficulties, but today many with previous experience are students with initiative who have deliberately sought opportunities to teach at home or overseas through VSO (Voluntary Service Overseas) or similar organisations.

Given the kind of background described in the researches outlined above, a number of enquiries have concentrated on selection procedures within the training institution. In one early piece of research Lawton (1939)[23] suggested 'estimates of character' as well as ratings of academic quality and extra-curricular interests as useful indicators of eventual success in the profession. His conclusions were based on a study of former students. Phillips (1953)[24] examined the use of English tests and IQ tests in considering students for training college, but his analysis of success in these showed little relation with eventual success in the college, and he obtained a better correlation with a projection test.

Burroughs (1958)[25] used factor analysis, as had Lovell (1951)[26] earlier, to investigate admission procedures, and reached the conclusion that the interview was as good a predictor of eventual success as most other measures 'provided that it was not expected to yield information beyond its powers'.[27] Final teaching marks were best predicted by ratings of observable features of the applicant, his powers of self-expression and intellectual maturity.

Halliwell (1965)[28] in the course of investigating the selection procedures in one college of education, supported Burroughs' finding that the college interview rating was the most successful means of selecting students. The predictive value of attitude and

49

personality tests varied according to the category of students under consideration. Since, of course, both the final teaching mark and the interview rating are given by the same group of people in these local enquiries, ie by college or university tutors, there is likely to be an element of self-fulfilling prophesy within any significant correlations obtained.

When Allen (1962)[29] took interview scores given to individual applicants and compared them with ratings from group interviews where groups of ten applicants took part in discussion with and without leaders, imaginary staff meetings etc, he found that the group interview ratings showed a better correlation with final teaching marks than individual interview ratings. This is an interesting finding which has been hardly followed up at all, possibly because of the administrative problem of both arranging group interviews and rating as many as ten candidates individually during the sessions.

Tarpey (1965)[30] looked at selection procedures in four Irish colleges, finding no relation between IQ test scores administered to new entrants and final teaching mark, and in only one of the four colleges a small correlation between some of the scores on the Cattell 16 PF Test and final teaching mark. More important, she found within the four colleges a considerable range of opinion among the tutors, there being substantial disagreement about what qualities were to be looked for in good teachers, and concluded that college tutors' opinions should not be regarded as reliable statistically.

Several of these studies, whilst of some interest, have few tangible implications for teacher training programmes. Isolated studies showing, for example, that some student teachers admired former teachers more than their own parents would need to be replicated in the training institutions concerned before they could be assumed to have relevance for students currently being prepared for teaching.

There are, however, some findings which do deserve consideration because they have been shown to exist at different times and under varying conditions. The middle-class background of many recruits, especially women graduates, means that they may be unfamiliar with the social conditions of a large percentage of the children they will teach. There is a strong case for them to gain experience of working with children from a wide variety of social backgrounds during training. Grant[31] has written about the six-week 'social practice' undertaken by trainee teachers in the Lower Saxony province of West Germany, and Floud has described the missionary role of many teachers in areas where their children suffer considerable deprivation:

> As long as we have slums or near slums (as in the negro-populated districts of the big northern cites of the US about which Conant has recently written, or in many areas of the European conurbations), teachers must be missionaries. But the missionary is a social worker; ought we perhaps in the affluent society to substitute the teacher-social worker for the teacher-missionary and reflect the new notion of his task in his education and training, grounding it firmly in the social and behavioural sciences?[32]

Courses for teacher-social workers do already exist, but it is not always possible for the ordinary student teacher to make normal contacts with working-class children except when this is specially arranged. Some possibilities will be considered in a later chapter, when projects such as that of Hannam, Smyth and Stephenson[33] at Bristol University will be described.

Students' motives for choosing teaching have been shown to vary, depending upon social and other conditions existing at any one time. A group which has chosen teaching for security, or for no apparent reason, may well need a different kind of approach from one which expresses love of children, or another, perhaps of secondary trainees, which claims attraction of specialist subject as its most powerful motivating factor.

One other area mentioned briefly above is worthy of comment at this stage, namely the potency of the teaching models to which the student has been exposed. It is often discovered that the students' own teachers have influenced them in their choice of career. What is less clearly evident from the research is the extent to which former models influence students' classroom behaviour. If one takes the secondary trainee as an example, he will, at a rough guess, have been exposed to something like 7,000 hours of secondary school teaching, assuming he has spent the customary seven years at school. If the style of teaching he received was predominantly information-giving, accompanied by little supplementary visual material or variety, it is hardly surprising that this is the model which most readily presents itself to him when he first tries his hand. Since many teacher training programmes are attempting to modify students' classroom behaviour, the effect of former models on the recruit's teaching habits are of critical importance.

ATTITUDES AND PERSONALITY

Several investigators have tried to measure students' attitudes during training. Some have concentrated on a purely local enquiry into the students' attitudes to their own course at a particular time, whereas others have tried to see how attitudes to education, or teaching or children change during or after training.

Thymme-Gouda (1948)[34] found students of four training colleges complaining somewhat about the course. They felt that teaching practice imposed a considerable strain on them, women expressing this opinion more than men. Possibly the atmosphere in a residential college in 1948 could have been more threatening than today. Later work has often substantiated Thymme-Gouda's findings, but sometimes contradicted them.

Charlton, Stewart and Paffard (1958)[35] were concerned with research into the early work in education at Keele University. Their sample of graduates welcomed teaching practice and felt training for it should be on sound theoretical principles. There was some similarity between these findings and those reported by Phillips (1931 and 1932)[36] (see p 68), though their use of a carefully constructed attitude scale was more sophisticated than Phillips' earlier enquiry.

When Shipman (1965)[37] investigated attitudes of various groups of student teachers in a training college, he discovered that the secondary teacher group was more academically oriented than the primary group. Earlier Steele (1958)[38] had also identified the expression of a more 'progressive' attitude among infant teacher trainees than junior. These findings suggest a steady continuum according to age-group being taught, ranging from a more child-centred attitude at one end, expressed by those preparing to teach the youngest children, to a more subject-centred attitude at the other end in those preparing for secondary school teaching. This view was also supported by Tudhope (1944) in the research reported above.

Williams (1963)[39] looked at the attitudes to their own training of a very large sample of student teachers, newly qualified teachers and experienced teachers. Student teachers ranked teaching practice as the most important part, whereas experienced teachers chose teaching methods. This research must be viewed with some caution, however, owing to the imbalance of the sample, which consisted of 1,736 student teachers, 222 newly qualified teachers and only twenty-four experienced teachers with ten or more years' teaching.

In the United States Davies (1969),[40] summarising recent American research into student teaching and the attitudes of the students, found also that teaching practice was the most strongly approved part of the course. Some writers, however, disagreed, and he quotes Iannacone and Button (1964) for the alternative point of view that teaching practice was a period when student teachers learned to get through lessons on time at the expense of engaging children in some significant enterprise.

Evans (1952)[41] found no correlation between attitude scores and final teaching mark, or between intelligence scores and final teaching mark when she administered tests to student teachers of four colleges and one department of education. She did find, however, that on her tests college students registered a more favourable attitude to teaching as a career than the postgraduate students.

A later study by Evans (1957)[42] was designed to measure student teachers' attitudes towards the actual day-to-day job of teaching. She constructed a test called 'A Teacher's Day', and found no correlation between scores on this test and final teaching mark. She did find a significant negative correlation between the interest scores and intelligent test scores, which led her to conclude: 'It is not the most intelligent who are most favourably inclined to teaching, and over-enthusiastic students should be regarded with suspicion.' This rather bold conclusion on thinly based research evidence certainly contradicts most of the research on teacher expectation and should be viewed with considerable caution by those involved in training students.

Another study by Evans (1958),[43] examining the Minnesota Teacher Attitude Inventory (MTAI), a test designed among other things to identify teachers who have good rapport with their children, found a correlation between the MTAI scores and theory marks but not teaching practice grades. The correlation between theory grades and MTAI scores, she suggests, could be due to the fact that liberal attitudes both score high on the test, and are likely to be rated highly by tutors marking theory papers in the present educational climate.

The whole question of American-based tests and the validity of American findings was faced in the cross-cultural investigation into the attitudes of over 2,000 American teacher trainees undertaken by the University of Toledo (1965).[44] Both the MTAI and Ryans' Teacher Characteristics measures (Ryans 1960)[45] were revised at the suggestion of the British advisory group. Contrary to popular expectation, British student teachers were rated more child-centred than their American counterparts on Ryans Characteristic B (learning-centred v child-centred). British students also scored higher on general intelligence and verbal comprehension, held less favourable attitudes to administration and school personnel, scored higher on tests of academic performance (except for elementary groups in science), and lower on 'measured areas of professional education' (tests on child development, instructional methods etc). As pointed out above, the high performance of English and Scottish graduates in the sample boosted the academic performance scores of the British sample. In any case it was difficult to get parallel samples in what were, in some respects, two quite different systems of training teachers.

Butcher (1965)[46] used attitude scales constructed at Manchester University to measure graduate students' naturalism (ie the attitude that children should be allowed to develop in their own way), radicalism and tender-mindedness. He found that students' scores on naturalism and radicalism increased during teacher training but that scores on all three attitude scales declined during the early years of teaching. The Manchester Opinion Scales were also used by McIntyre and Morrison (1967)[47] who recorded a similar increase in scores on the three scales during training by both graduate and non-graduate student teachers. After one year of teaching, a group of non-graduates who were followed up showed a decline in scores on all three measures. Only infants' school teachers held their scores steady on the naturalism scale.

Evans (1967)[48] reported significantly increased MTAI scores both for men and women students during the training year when she administered the MTAI to a sample of seventy-eight post-graduate students at the beginning and end of their course. Scores on the Allport Study of Values Test, however, remained fairly constant. American research using the MTAI to measure attitude change during or after training now runs to a number of studies. Rabinowitz and Rosenbaum (1959)[49] found a decline in MTAI scores after three years of teaching experience, and Scott and Brinkley (1960),[50] in an interesting investigation which took MTAI scores for cooperating teachers supervising the students as well as the students' scores, found that students working alongside teachers who scored higher than themselves on the MTAI showed higher scores after teaching practice, and those working with teachers scoring lower than themselves produced no change. Scott and Brinkley's findings make a valuable contribution to knowledge of attitude formation by pointing out the role of the cooperating teacher in influencing attitudes.

The area of attitude change is one in which most of the research agrees. Broadly speaking, attitudes show a movement towards child-centredness during training, this movement being influenced by the views held or believed to be held by the tutors of the training establishment, or by the cooperating teachers. After the training period, attitudes become more similar to those current in the school, as research quoted below will also show.

One final piece of research in this area by the present writer (Wragg 1967)[51] looked at students' attitudes to discipline. This enquiry involved asking ninety postgraduate students to rank ten common forms of indiscipline in school, such as children carving initials on a desk, reading obscene books etc, on a four-point scale indicating the severity with which they were viewed. The students also rated these forms of indiscipline as they believed their former teachers would have rated them. In every case their own ratings were less severe than those they attributed to their former school, but the rank order of the 'offences' was very similar.

Much of the research into the area of personality has involved attempts to correlate personality variables, as measured by standardised tests, with teaching success. Cortis (1968)[52] used creativity tests as well as personality tests and related the scores to practical teaching grades, theory marks and academic subject marks in college of education students. He concluded that 'grades on practical teaching did not correlate significantly with any of the cognitive variables, which may indicate that teaching skill bears no direct relationship to cognitive ability.'[53] It is difficult to accept this conclusion, even though it is tentatively expressed. As most trainees score relatively high on tests of cognitive strength, statistical artifacts tend to result.

An attempt to discriminate between college students rated as 'good' (A or B teaching mark) and those rated 'poor' (D or E teaching mark) was made by Herbert and Turnbull (1963).[54] They found no significant difference between the two groups on personality variables as measured by personality tests. Their only positive results were for MTAI scores, which, they concluded, best separated the two groups. They also noted a gradual increase in MTAI scores over 3 years, and found that MTAI scores were related to theory marks in education and to psychology marks.

Mann (1961)[55] used a large battery of tests of personality, intelligence, habits and attitudes, as well as biographical questionnaires and interviews, in an attempt to identify the factors influencing success in a teacher training college. His sample consisted of 40 men and 40 women spread evenly over the different year groups. He found significant correlations between teaching practice success and a number of variables, including good financial status of family, level and length of education of mother, physical stature and bearing, and, of the personality variables, vitality and dependability. This is a well planned and thorough study which should be replicated under present conditions.

Warburton, Butcher and Forrest (1963)[56] investigated 118 volunteers out of 133 postgraduate certificate students at Manchester University Department of Education. Final data were assembled for 100 students on 100 variables (57 test scores, 25 biographical variables and 18 criteria of success). Some of the Cattell 16 PF scores were among the best predictors of success in teaching practice, notably conscientiousness, sensitivity and self-control. As in earlier research quoted above, interview grade showed a positive correlation with final teaching mark. This is a substantial enquiry into teaching success, but despite the positive correlations with some personality variables, the writers conclude:

It would, therefore, appear best in selecting potential teachers to concentrate on attainment and general culture rather than on extraversion or introversion, on academic rather than aesthetic interests, and on participation in social activities rather than social or domestic background.[57]

They also make the important point that the group tested is in fact a successful group which does not include those rejected at interview. Were the whole group of applicants to be tested, they argue, the significance of many of the correlations would probably be strengthened.

As can be seen from the above, studies of student teachers' personalities are sparse, usually involve other variables, and rarely correlate with measures of teaching effectiveness. Since, subjectively, many would report that students' success in the classroom *is* dependent on their personality, there seems to be a great need for further research. Only the work of Mann (1961) and Warburton, Butcher and Forrest (1963), of the research described above, comes near to making any significant contribution in this area.

Students' personality and attitudes are of central importance in teacher training. A great deal of effort is devoted to analysing and modifying attitudes and consequently, it is hoped, behaviour, and this can scarcely be undertaken in a climate of total unawareness of the nature of students' attitudes and the direction of attitude change. The study of attitudes and attitude change can be a barren one, because one tends to assume a certain congruence between stated attitudes and actual classroom behaviour. Yet it might be wrong to infer, for example, that students whose attitude scores become more child-centred during training will show greater warmth and concern for individual children in their classes. They may indeed do so, but it is not inevitable.

Personality is of concern, since certain personality types might make more effective teachers than others. At the moment there is no clear evidence that they do, and studies which have used instruments like the Cattell 16 PF have often contradicted each other with their findings. Even if, for example, extraversion were consistently shown to be related to effective teaching as rated by supervisors, this might only reflect a general preference of supervisors for extravert teachers. The section below will show that the colossal amount of research into teacher effectiveness has only underlined the amount of doubt and disagreement which exists about what constitutes good teaching.

If teacher training is partly concerned with the modification of behaviour, personality theory should be applied more in relation to behaviour change than measures of effectiveness. What is of primary importance is who is likely to change or not change during and after various kinds of training. One study of experienced teachers participating in an in-service workshop showed that teachers scoring high on certain personality traits, such as the psychopathic deviate and schizophrenia scales of the Minnesota Multiphasic Personality Inventory, were less likely to change their classroom behaviour as a result of the course.[58] Other investigators have studied the open/closed mindedness phenomenon to see who is likely or unlikely to modify his behaviour in the light of training.

TEACHING PRACTICE AND THE RELEVANT RESEARCH INTO TEACHER EFFECTIVENESS

Several of the studies mentioned so far in this review attempted to relate variables of one kind or another to what they called 'success' in teaching practice, and almost inevitably this has meant final teaching practice mark as given by the training institution. Since the procedures for defining 'success' are varied, it is worth looking at what constitutes teaching effectiveness.

In many training institutions the final teaching mark is the assessment of one supervising tutor, unendorsed by the observations of others; in some there is double rating by internal and external assessors; and in others there is a composite rating by the school personnel, internal tutors and external assessors. When she surveyed current methods of assessing teachers' competence, Evans (1951) concluded that the best criterion of effectiveness would be 'a composite measure based on pupil gains in information, ratings by competent observers, and a rating based upon opinions of pupils'.[59]

An American writer, Barr (1961), summarising a massive amount of American research into teacher effectiveness, pointed out: 'Some teachers were preferred by administrators, some were liked by the pupils, and some taught in classes where there were substantial pupil gains, and generally speaking these were not the same teachers.'[60]

In other words there is comparatively little agreement among researchers about one single criterion of good teaching, and studies which have taken pupil gains on achievement tests, and pupil or observer ratings, have produced quite different groups of 'good' teachers. There is not even agreement between different observers rating the same teacher, as Barr went on to point out:

> There is plenty of evidence to indicate that different practitioners observing the same teacher teach, or studying data about her, may arrive at very different evaluations of her; this observation is equally true of the evaluation experts; starting with different approaches, and using different data-gathering devices, they, too, arrive at very different evaluations.[61]

More research will be quoted below to illustrate Barr's point about different evaluators seeing the same teacher differently. In any case the evaluator, who is usually in a position of authority, as Anderson and Hunka (1968)[62] point out, is likely to find that to some extent the teaching may be aimed at him rather than at the class.

Few studies use pupil ratings of effectiveness. None of the published studies of student teaching in this country has taken pupil ratings as criteria of effectiveness. In a huge survey of 672 studies of teacher effectiveness reported by Domas and Tiedeman (1950)[63] only seven used pupil ratings.

One good example of the state of disagreement, even among researchers working with similar groups of teachers at the same time, is shown in the conflicting reports of Rostker (1945) and Rolfe (1945). Both investigated large samples of teachers, used standardised observation and testing techniques, yet, on reporting their findings, Rostker concluded, 'The intelligence of the teacher is the highest single factor conditioning teaching ability and remains so even when in combination with other teacher measures. Personality, as here defined and measured, shows no significant relationship to teaching ability';[64] whereas Rolfe said, 'Intelligence as measured by the American Council Psychological examination seems not to be related to teaching efficiency (r $= -0.10$).'[65]

One early attempt to identify common criteria in rating both experienced and trainee teachers was Cattell's (1931)[66] survey of the opinions of inspectors, training college lecturers, heads, teachers and pupils. The respondents were asked to identify the ten most important traits of the good experienced teacher and the good young teacher. Cattell isolated twenty-two traits from the replies, the qualities of a good young teacher differing only slightly from those expected of a good mature teacher. Personality and will, and intelligence came highest on the list. This piece of research, less primitive in construction than most similar work in the early 1930s, produced a greater measure of agreement between the various groups about criteria of good teaching than has been the case subsequently.

Biddle and Ellena (1964)[67] describe how some investigators prefer to study teachers' *behaviour* and others their *properties* in attempts to identify effective teaching. In the same book Davis points out that because of the difficulty of identifying effective teaching, the use of rating forms in the United States declined from 82 per cent of large systems using them in 1923 to only 35 per cent by 1955. Again in the same book Rosenkrantz and Biddle describe the Kansas City role studies which showed that there was no clear agreement about the role the teacher should play among those concerned with education. Because of this lack of definition it was difficult to decide how effectively the teacher was doing his job. Moreover, the Kansas research found that officials erected a falsely stereotyped consensus role for teachers as conservative guardians of moral values which they claimed society wanted, though they could find no sector of society which would admit to expecting that role to be fulfilled.

In the face of his international confusion about what constitutes good teaching it is hardly surprising, then, that most studies of British student teachers have settled for final teaching practice mark as a criterion of effectiveness, however frail a criterion it may be.

One interesting hypothesis was tested by Cornwell (1958).[68] He argued that since it was important for teachers to get on well with people, there ought to be some correlation between the degree to which they get on with each other in training and their success in the classroom. He gave a series of sociometric tests to seventy-three students in the second term of a 2-year course at a residential training college and found that the scores they obtained correlated 0.57 with final teaching practice mark nearly $1\frac{1}{2}$ years later. Since the enquiry was conducted in the residential training college, it could be argued that tutor-given grades might also merely reflect the tutors' own partiality to popular students. However, this research offers interesting possibilities, and deserves to be replicated on a wider scale and under modern conditions.

Griffiths and Moore (1967)[69] circularised the heads of twenty teaching practice schools representing a wide variety of the schools used by a college of education. They concluded that the schools saw the training of teachers as peripheral to their own task. None of these schools had ever discussed teaching practice at a staff meeting. Although nineteen out of twenty heads showed little or no knowledge of what happened in the college, twelve of them thought college teaching was 'unrealistic' and that supervision by college staff was inadequate.

In an attempt to test Barr's conclusion described above that, by and large, evaluators disagree about the same teacher, the present writer (Wragg 1968)[70] set up a situation where thirty-five tutors from two colleges, one institute and one department of education watched and rated a lesson given by a student teacher on videotape. Subsequently, when the tutors filled in evaluation forms and held a discussion of the lesson, there was little agreement either in written responses to questions on the evaluation sheet or in open discussion. The rating of the lesson ranged from B+ to D.

Similarly, when Robertson (1957)[71] asked eighteen supervisors experienced in the training of graduate students to list fifty attributes in order of priority, he found they showed little agreement with each other. Correlation between the eighteen sets of ratings ranged from 0.73 to − 0.16, with a coefficient of concordance of + 0.38.

Poppleton (1968)[72] investigated the measure of agreement between schools and tutors in the Sheffield University Department of Education. Analysis of rating forms on 249 student teachers showed a correlation of 0.60. To some extent school and tutor ratings are not arrived at totally independently, as tutors and supervising teachers will usually consult and influence each other's thinking throughout the course of a normal teaching practice.

Cohen (1965)[73] found that there was little agreement between tutors and student teachers on the question of teachers' behaviour in the classroom. Later Finlayson and Cohen (1967)[74] found that heads of teaching practice schools rated the maintenance of good order and discipline more highly than the growth and mental well-being of individual children, whereas student teachers, particularly second-year college students, felt the reverse. The writer described the second-year students' views as coming at a time when students could afford to demonstrate 'maximal liberality'.

One piece of research concerned itself with the effect of teaching practice placing on students' assessment. Collier (1959)[75] asked college tutors to rank schools according to how difficult they were to teach in. Subsequent analysis of teaching marks given to students who had taught in those schools identified as 'difficult' by the tutors showed an average teaching mark of between C and C — as opposed to an average of B — to C + in other schools. The highest teaching mark given in the 'difficult' schools had been B +. Since the college had made special efforts to keep known 'weak' students out of the tougher schools, the influence of teaching practice placing on teaching mark is even more pronounced.

In the United States Joyce and Harootunian (1964)[76] questioned student teachers on teaching practice to discover how they determined their objectives, planned their lessons etc. They concluded that nearly all the decision-making processes had little to do with rationalised educational theory. Lessons rarely had objectives, and methods were intuitively arrived at and were not choices from alternatives. Most lessons were reflections of the cooperating teacher and of practice in the teaching practice school. The writers inferred from their observations that students tended to borrow the practices they saw rather than create original tactics.

Once more in the United States McGrath (1950)[77] investigated problems facing students on teaching practice. He used a checklist of difficulties mentioned by student teachers in the past and asked the respondents to check those which applied to them. He found that student teachers stressed problems such as adjusting to individual needs, getting to know children well, getting children to work, and lack of time for consultation with experienced teachers or the cooperating teacher. Much of this was supported by the present writer (Wragg 1967), who found that students' greatest hope for teaching practice was to be able to arouse and hold interest, and the greatest anxiety was over class control.

Collier (1957)[78] studied reports of group discussions and diaries kept by first-year students at St Luke's College, Exeter. He found that students were extremely apprehensive before their first teaching practice and that failure on teaching practice caused a considerable loss of self-respect. Other points which emerged were a certain anxiety when tutors were present in the room and a degree of disillusionment about the experienced teachers the students had met during their teaching practice.

Tibble (1959)[79] found that three-quarters of the student teachers in his sample worried about discipline and class control. Half had anxieties about subject matter. Only a tiny number felt after the practice was over that their anxieties had been realised on the scale they had feared, though half said the difficulties they had anticipated had materialised, but on a smaller scale than they had envisaged.

Some investigators have looked at supervision of teaching practice. Baker (1967),[80] for example, describes the teacher-tutor scheme, which seeks to bring teachers directly into the teacher training situation along the lines of the cooperating teacher in the United States.

Adaptations of some of the techniques used to train social workers are reported by Caspari and Eggleston (1965).[81] In this situation supervising tutors do not visit schools, the students report back to their tutors about what has happened in the classroom. To some extent this is open to distortion, but the presence of a tutor in the classroom may also significantly alter what usually happens. Certainly this approach is worth considering in more detail. At present it has received only qualitative evaluation. Further experiments along these lines are reported by Clark (1967)[82] at St Gabriel's College, London.

Little has been done on optimum length of school practice. ATCDE (1962)[83] reached the conclusion that there was no evidence that 12 weeks teaching practice was better than 6. The National Union of Teachers (1970)[84] reports that a conference of comprehensive school heads preferred the long block practice on the lines used by many university departments of education to shorter practices.

Cope (1971)[85] also investigated the question of length of teaching practice in a thorough study which solicited the opinion of students, supervisors and teachers. She listed the frustrations of each of the three groups canvassed, and found that all felt that teaching practice was too short. Students were also anxious about assessment procedures.

The Exeter Enquiry

Most of the research so far described has concentrated on describing teaching practice by students' responses to questionnaires. The Exeter Enquiry (Wragg 1972)[86] was a study of 102 graduate student teachers based on an analysis of 578 lessons observed and recorded by a team of trained observers. It is fully described elsewhere, but some of the findings are of particular relevance to teacher training.

It was found that most students had relatively fixed patterns of teaching, showing slight changes in style from lesson to lesson, while only a small number had very varied patterns. Subject being taught was the most powerful determinant of teaching style, and the various subjects observed tended to have regular and fairly predictable teaching styles associated with them. Only English teachers as a group showed very varied patterns of classroom interaction. The successful student tended to be well qualified academically, have an enthusiastic, unconventional and experimenting personality, be flexible in his working, use little criticism of pupils, and solicit frequent pupil response.

These findings and the ones described above are probably of greater importance to teacher training than research described in other areas. Of prime concern is the frequent lack of agreement between evaluation experts and others on the qualities required by the good teacher. The reporting of such enquiries is perhaps one-sided, in that investigators are less likely to rush to publish research which merely shows that raters do agree with each other. Nevertheless the whole area of teacher effectiveness research only serves to highlight disagreements within the profession. Recently Stones and Morris (1972)[87] have again described the largely idiosyncratic nature of assessment of student teachers on practice. After long periods in history when there was not a great deal of conflict about the nature of good teaching, we have relatively little harmony. This suggests that students must be pressed more in the direction of self-evaluation and self-determined behaviour modification, and this is an important theme for the rest of this book.

The second area of concern is the question of student anxiety, which is constantly reported by investigators. The implication of this is not that assessment procedures should cease to exist, as historically the advent of certification by a group of responsible people rather than a system of personal patronage by an individual has led to a considerable strengthening of the profession. The questions raised by studies of student anxiety concern much more the issue of performance. Too much anxiety tends to impair performance, as may too little. Anxiety induced by pressures to please a superior or teacher whose own criteria may well be unclear and unsupported by others is compounded by the other sources of anxiety about classroom relations, discipline and subject matter. Excessive anxiety may prevent real learning or more permanent change of behaviour from taking place.

Thirdly there is the question of pressure on schools and how students best learn to teach. Price (1964)[88] has discussed the crisis stage which has been reached in school practice. He suggested the exploration of methods such as closed-circuit television, team teaching and college-linked schools. It will again be a concern of much of this book to explore some of the alternatives to conventional school practice, but not in any sense, it must be stressed, to replace it. The purpose of micro-teaching and other kinds of experience with children should be to enable students to derive maximum benefit from their longer periods of practice by ensuring they are more competent and confident when they begin them than has often been the case hitherto.

FOLLOW-UP STUDIES OF FORMER STUDENTS

The last area of research into teacher training to be surveyed consists of a number of studies which have followed up former students. Some of these studies have measured their attitude change or their behaviour change, while others have attempted to get measures of their competence in the classroom and relate these to various measures taken at the time of training.

Shipman (1967),[89] accepting the weakness of the attitude questionnaire, which often produces answers which the student feels the tester wants, used one to measure teachers' attitudes to teaching six months after they had left college. As with other

66

studies quoted above, he found the students' expressed attitudes were no longer similar to those of the college staff but had moved towards the ones expressed by the majority of teachers in the schools.

A study by Collins (1964)[90] attempted to measure the effects of training by following up a group of graduates trained at Leicester University Department of Education and comparing them with a group of untrained graduates matched for sex, degree class and degree subject. She found that the untrained teachers were rated lower by the heads, were more likely to be absent from school and for longer periods, were less likely to read professional journals or join a professional association, were more likely to have their probationary year extended, and were more likely to leave the profession altogether. Because of possible differences in motivation of the two groups, it is difficult to draw firm inferences from what Collins described, but at least there was some indication that trained graduates showed a greater degree of competence and interest than untrained graduates.

A different approach to measuring the effects of training was used by Turner (1963)[91] in the United States. He used a test which had been shown to be correlated with pupil gains over a period of two years. Training in methods courses and a period of teaching practice produced higher scores from the student teacher on Turner's tests, from which Turner inferred that it was now more likely that the student teachers would produce more pupil achievement gains. The scores of individual students showed significant correlation with the scores of their cooperating teachers, and there were disproportionate gains in scores according to the training establishment the student had attended. The whole of Turner's conclusions hinge on the validity of his test, but if his test *is* valid, it would suggest that both the training in the institution and the work of the cooperating teacher have a measurable effect in increasing student teachers' competence.

Clark and Nisbet (1963)[92] followed up a group of teachers who had left a Scottish college 2 years previously. Reacting to their training course, these teachers, especially the graduates, reported that teaching practice had been the most useful part of the course.

The writers observed that the students questioned saw their training primarily as a matter of learning techniques, and regarded many other things as a waste of time.

One by-product of the Rudd and Wiseman (1962)[93] investigation of sources of dissatisfaction among experienced teachers was that, although their chief complaints were about their salaries, working conditions, status and class size, rather than the training they had received, there was some evidence that they would have preferred more school practice and more emphasis on methods of teaching in their training for the profession.

In an early piece of pioneer research Phillips (1931 and 1932)[94] followed up a number of her former students in an attempt to discover their problems, so that her findings might inform those engaged in training teachers. The main problems reported were not unlike those of the student teacher, and concerned mainly discipline, class management, and relations with older teachers in the school. Students reported that they had found the teaching practice and theory elements of their training course to be complementary. They would have appreciated more help with discipline, and they had found educational psychology the most valuable part of the theory course.

There are a number of follow-up studies which look at ratings of effectiveness. In the United States Bach (1952)[95] found no correlation between ratings made by teaching practice supervisors and those made by principals of schools only 4 months after the students had taken up their first teaching post.

A smaller sample of college students followed up in this country by Pearce (1959)[96] in their first year of teaching produced some interesting observations. Only forty students were involved, but Pearce concluded that personal qualities or a favourable or unfavourable environment could significantly influence their performance in their first post.

By far the highest correlation between final teaching practice mark and follow-up ratings were achieved by Tudhope (1942 and 1943).[97] He looked at ratings by HMIs of ninety-six teachers who had taught for at least 3 years and compared them with the final college teaching mark. The median length of teaching experience of his sample was 9 years. His calculations showed a correlation between the two sets of scores of 0.84 for men and 0.77 in the case of women. This is very much higher than any other correlation reported in the literature. As has been pointed out above, there was formerly much greater agreement about what constituted effective teaching than there is now. It should also be mentioned that HMIs shared in the original college ratings, that the purpose of Tudhope's enquiry was to counter criticisms of the procedure for awarding teaching grades, and that the ninety-six teachers, and presumably something of their college records, were also usually known by the raters. Nevertheless such high agreement is supported by no other study.

The nearest correlation to Tudhope's from a follow-up enquiry was reported by Collins (1959),[98] who compared heads' ratings on a 9-point scale of 115 former graduate student teachers with teaching practice grades. A bi-serial correlation of 0.566 was obtained.

Wiseman and Start (1965)[99] have reported a follow-up of 248 former students who qualified in 1955 at seven colleges and one university department in the Manchester area. Unfortunately the response rate was low (36 per cent of the sample), which may be responsible for a certain amount of distortion, and the findings obviously cannot give the fuller picture which a higher response rate could provide; nevertheless the indications are that there is only a low correlation between ratings of competence at the training stage and a number of criteria of success in the profession, such as heads' reports, promotion achieved etc.

There is little evidence about weaker students once they leave. Collins (1969)[100] describes a follow-up of former students in their first post. She found that on the whole students who had been given a D teaching mark were getting extra help in their schools. Although the heads in her sample felt that they were usually helpful to probationer teachers, the probationers themselves reported getting very little help from heads. Most of the help they received came from heads of departments and other teachers.

Earlier Edmonds (1966)[101] analysed reasons why some students had had their probationary year extended. He found the chief

69

reasons were poor class management and basic inability to secure discipline, particularly at secondary level.

The follow-up over the longest period of time reported in the literature was by Nisbet (1954).[102] He took a sample of 335 students who had qualified as teachers between 1930 and 1934 and looked at them 20 years later. Final data on 222 of these produced information about teaching posts held which could be related to intelligence test scores, practical teaching mark, a general college assessment, and degree class available from the subjects' records as students. The only significant correlations between status in the teaching profession, ie degree of promotion achieved, and the scores at the training stage were $+ 0.36$ with degree class and $+ 0.26$ with intelligence. Clearly the nature of the promotion system is such as to ensure a relatively high correlation with degree class.

Many of these studies have importance for the in-service education of teachers, especially those which show reasons for lack of success, such as failure to maintain classroom order during the probationary year. A comprehensive system of in-service education can maintain contact with new teachers, and those known to be at risk can be given special help. There is a need for further exploration of the hardening of attitudes of students in their first years of teaching. Does regular full-time teaching inevitably sour ideals? Are high ideals and reality irreconcilable?

As far as initial student teaching programmes are concerned there is again evidence that longer teaching practice is preferred. The difficulties of classroom management experienced by some probationer teachers in their first year suggests that post-teaching practice remedial work is of vital importance in colleges. This is an area which tends to be neglected, but it is one where many of the techniques, such as micro-teaching, although they may be of primary utility before teaching practice, can still be of value at the end of a course in the light of known weaknesses.

For notes to this chapter see pp 197-204.

3 Interaction Analysis

Studies of classrooms based on live observation of the teachers and children in them were few in number before 1960. Since then, however, there has been a substantial increase in research analysing classroom processes in the United States, Britain and numerous other countries.

The findings of such studies are of considerable importance to both experienced and novice teachers, but only in certain respects. As one would expect from the studies of teacher effectiveness described in Chapter 2, no universally 'good' patterns of teaching have emerged. Despite the tireless efforts of several investigators to identify classroom styles which might be shown to produce consistent gains in learning, improvement in children's attitudes to school or high efficiency ratings from observers, little has emerged. Rosenshine, analysing over fifty studies in which observed teacher behaviour was related to measures of children's learning, including research ino the use of praise and criticism, organising skill, variety of teaching pattern and clarity, came to the conclusion that, even though some findings showed a certain consistency (eg twelve out of seventeen investigators found negative correlations between teachers' use of criticism and children's learning), it would be wrong to develop a checklist of 'good' strategies on the basis of the evidence so far available:

First, student achievement is inadequate as a *sole* measure of teacher effectiveness; second, the results of these studies can be seen only as tentative ideas which are worthy of further study. We simply have not conducted enough research on teaching to enable us to develop observational checklists which can be applied to teachers with any confidence.[1]

This simply adds to the evidence that student teachers should not be moulded in any predetermined shape. The relevance of interaction analysis is that it can make the new teacher more aware of classroom processes and also give him a greater measure of control over that part of his behaviour which is open to his own manipulation. During a conventional teaching practice assignment students experience tens of thousands of classroom episodes. Jackson[2] spent a sabbatical year observing teachers in their classrooms as an anthropologist might, and noted that as many as a thousand interpersonal transactions would be completed by a teacher in one day.

Student teachers learn a great deal from their interactions with children during teaching practice, but they might learn even more if they took the time to subject some of their own teaching behaviour to careful scrutiny. Joyce and Harootunian,[3] as mentioned in Chapter 2, were sceptical both about the quality of student teachers' self-analysis and their ability to control their own behaviour. They found that the students' teaching methods were arrived at intuitively and not consciously chosen from alternatives. Moreover the strategies employed tended to mirror those current in the teaching practice school.

The writer's own study of student teachers at Leicester University[4] revealed that student teachers, while consciously *rejecting* certain aspects of the teaching they themselves received at school and witnessed at their teaching practice school, and while *wishing* to make changes, often found themselves unable to control their own classroom behaviour when faced by a group of children, even where these were being totally cooperative. The writer's own subsequent study of 102 student teachers at Exeter University[5] also showed that many students had fairly fixed patterns of teaching with little variety from one lesson to the next. Wallen and Travers[6] in their description of studies of experienced American teachers found a similarly limited range of strategies being employed by several teachers, who frequently imitated the traditional models to which they themselves had been exposed.

If it is the case that students tend to copy the familiar, then there is clearly a danger that current practices, however good or bad, may be propagated indefinitely with only minimal changes. The purpose of putting trainee teachers in a position where they must scrutinise their own classroom behaviour is twofold: firstly it can make them aware of rigidity, inflexibility or limitations in their teaching, and secondly it can offer them a measure of control and a certain degree of release from their traditional dependence on tutors and supervising teachers for objective analysis of the processes in their classrooms.

WHAT INTERACTION ANALYSIS IS

There are many systems for analysing classroom processes, some more suitable for student teachers than others. Simon and Boyer have published a seventeen-volume collection of systems[7] and research findings which is by no means complete, even though it describes ninety-two different methods of analysis, many of which are in current use. Numerous unpublished systems exist, and indeed devising and applying one's own schedule is an interesting and illuminating task both for the experienced and novice teacher. Medley and Mitzel[8] have written at length about principles of designing category systems, and their guidelines and warnings are extremely useful to anyone undertaking the exercise for the first time.

Among the earliest attempts to analyse and describe in a systematic way the spontaneous interaction between a teacher and the children in her class was the work of Anderson,[9] who, from as early as 1939, observed for a number of years the sort of 'contacts' between children in nursery and elementary school classes, and related these to the behaviour of the teacher towards the children. He regularly found that the teacher who was 'dominative' would have more dominative contacts between the children in her class, ie snatching toys, striking playmates, giving commands to others, whereas the 'integrative' teacher would find more integrative acts in his classroom, such as sharing toys, offering help and playing harmoniously.

Soon after Anderson's early work Lippitt[10] and later White, working with Kurt Lewin, carried out their well known research into the effects of adult leaders' behaviour on groups of five boys engaged in various activities. Despite the shortcomings of this pioneer research, including its partial irrelevance to school classes of much larger size, the concept of children's dependence on the leader shown by Anderson clearly came through. The presence or absence of the leaders, who played authoritarian, democratic and laissez-faire roles, produced different patterns of behaviour from the boys. The absence of the authoritarian-type leader, for example, led to acts of aggression by the group, whereas the democratic leader's group functioned in what Anderson would have called an integrative way, whether the leader was there or not. Much of this early work must be seen against the historical background of World War II, where the pressure was to show that a democratic teaching style was more desirable than an authoritarian one.

Withall (1949)[11] was among the first to develop a formal category system. His classification of the teacher's verbal statements into seven categories showed a pattern of teacher *verbal* behaviour similar to that produced by Anderson's categorisation of *general* behaviour.

From these early studies it was becoming clear that since it was not possible to record every detail of what happened in a class, it was best to concentrate on a particular aspect. More and more research was devoted to teacher *talk*. Flanders[12] developed a 10 category system for categorising talk by both teacher and children. After many hours of live classroom observation he formulated his 'rule of two-thirds'. Of all the lessons he observed, roughly two-thirds consisted of talk. Two-thirds of this talk was by the teacher, and two-thirds of the teacher's talk was devoted to giving information. Flanders argued that talk was highly correlated with behaviour, and that spontaneous verbal interaction between teachers and children should therefore be subjected to systematic analysis.

THE FLANDERS SYSTEM

It is worth considering the Flanders system in some detail, as it has been widely applied, is often used in modified form, and can

THE 10 CATEGORIES

	1	Accepts feeling: accepts and clarifies the feeling tone of the student in a non-threatening manner. Feelings may be positive or negative. Predicting and recalling feelings are included.
Indirect influence	2	Praises or encourages: praises or encourages student action or behaviour. Jokes that release tension, not at the expense of another individual, nodding head or saying 'uh huh?' or 'go on' are included.
	3	Accepts or uses ideas of student: clarifying, building or developing ideas or suggestions by a student. As teacher brings more of his own ideas into play, shift to category five.
	4	Asks questions: asking a question about content or procedure with the intent that a student answer.

Teacher talk

	5	Lectures: giving facts or opinions about content or procedure; expressing his own idea; asking rhetorical questions.
Direct influence	6	Gives directions: directions, commands, or orders with which a student is expected to comply.
	7	Criticises or justifies authority: statements, intended to change student behaviour from non-acceptable to acceptable pattern; bawling someone out; stating why the teacher is doing what he is doing, extreme self-reference.

Student talk	8	Student talk-response: talk by students in response to teacher. Teacher initiates the contact or solicits student statement.
	9	Student talk-initiation: talk by students which they initiate. If 'calling on' student is only to indicate who may talk next, the observer must decide whether student wanted to talk. If he did, use this category.

	10	Silence or confusion: pauses, short periods of silence, and periods of confusion in which communication cannot be understood by the observer.

serve as an illustration of the use and misuse of interaction analysis as a teacher training technique. It extends earlier work described above by dividing verbal activity into 10 categories each of which has a number. There is no scale implied by the numbers. See p 75.

Categories 1 to 4, which Flanders calls 'Indirect influence', correspond roughly to Anderson's 'integrative' concept, and categories 5, 6 and 7, where to some extent the teacher is limiting the verbal activity of the class, correspond approximately to his 'dominative' concept. It is not necessary to use the concepts of directness and indirectness, as these terms do to some extent have value connotations, in that it would be easy to associate indirectness with child-centred, democratic, 'good' teaching, and direct teaching with undesirable overtones. Since all teachers use both styles at some stages the terms are not likely to be helpful to the trainee.

The procedures for using the Flanders system are quite straightforward and have been fully described elsewhere by Flanders.[13] An observer watches a teacher during a lesson, and every three seconds he writes down the category number of the interaction he has just observed. He records these numbers in sequence in a column, writing approximately twenty numbers per minute, so that after, say, 25 minutes, he will have a sequence of approximately 500 numbers. The observer has first been trained for several hours from tapes, videotapes and live situations, if possible, until he shows considerable agreement with other trained observers. Inter-observer agreement can be calculated by a formula suggested by Scott[14] and it takes only 10 or 12 hours of training to produce inter-observer agreements of 0.8 or above. If, of course, the activity is not appropriate, eg a film being shown, everyone working in silence, or if the observer cannot hear, then he stops tallying.

Recording lessons

Suppose, for example, a teacher comes into the class and says, 'Open your books at the map on page 60', then the observer writes 6, signifying a command. If the teacher then goes on to

ask, 'What is the country coloured green?' the observer writes a
4. If silence follows the question, he writes a 10, and when someone replies, 'I think it's Finland, but I'm not sure', he writes 8.
Now the sequence of command, question, silence, answer is shown
by the observer's set of four numbers 6 – 4 – 10 – 8.

When the observer has collected several hundred such tallies
he needs to be able to present these to the teacher in an under-
standable form. One way obviously is to give the totals of each
category as a percentage of the whole, so that a teacher can see
how much praise he uses, how much spontaneous talk by the
children occurs, or how much use of questioning he makes. But
more interesting is an analysis of the actual sequence of the events.
For example, questions may always be followed by silence, or
sequences such as 4 – 8 – 4 – 8 – 4 – 8 – 4 – 8 will show rapid
question and answer, almost like drill.

	1	2	3	4	5	6	7	8	9	10
1										
2										
3										
4										1
5										
6				1						
7										
8										
9										
10								1		

Fig 1   10 × 10 matrix showing sequence 6 – 4 – 10 – 8 tallied in three cells

77

A particularly interesting way of displaying data is to compile a 10 × 10 matrix. To do this the numbers are taken in pairs and put into the appropriate cell. If one takes the sequence given above 6 – 4 – 10 – 8, the first pair of numbers is 6 – 4, ie command followed by question, so the tally goes into the 6 – 4 cell (counting *down* 6, *across* 4), as shown in Figure 1. The next pair is 4 – 10 (each number is the second of the previous pair and the first of the next pair), the third pair 10 – 8 and so on.

The student teacher can gain all kinds of insights into his lessons from the data collected. Flanders[15] has described how flow chart analysis can be used to highlight the predominant styles of teaching adopted by the teachers. Figs 2 and 3 show the matrices of two students teaching in similar circumstances. Both were female students in girls' grammar schools in the same city. They

-	1	2	3	4	5	6	7	8	9	10	Total
1	6	0	0	7	4	1	0	1	3	8	31
2	0	1	1	1	0	0	0	0	5	1	10
3	2	1	8	10	6	2	0	1	5	8	42
4	0	0	1	18	5	1	0	54	3	15	98
5	3	0	1	15	93	4	0	3	9	10	139
6	0	0	0	2	3	5	1	5	3	8	27
7	0	0	0	0	0	0	0	0	1	3	4
8	8	1	15	12	5	4	0	124	16	10	195
9	9	6	12	13	7	3	0	1	173	26	249
10	3	0	4	21	15	7	3	7	30	115	205
										Total	1000

Fig 2   English lessons given by Teacher A

78

	1	2	3	4	5	6	7	8	9	10	Total
1	0	0	0	0	0	0	0	0	0	0	0
2	0	0	0	1	2	0	0	1	0	1	6
3	0	3	1	17	38	1	0	0	1	10	71
4	0	0	0	30	8	2	2	86	0	26	154
5	0	0	1	66	321	13	1	3	10	16	431
6	0	0	0	3	10	13	0	1	0	11	38
7	0	0	0	3	0	0	5	0	1	3	13
8	0	2	63	13	18	2	2	5	3	7	115
9	0	0	7	2	7	1	1	0	5	2	25
10	0	0	0	19	27	7	1	13	5	71	147
										Total	1000

Fig 3   Geography lessons given by Teacher B

had been observed for six lessons during their teaching practice (some three hours of teaching time) and approximately 3,600 Flanders tallies were taken. These have been reduced to a common base of 1,000 (called a millage matrix) so that certain comparisons may be made.

Teacher A was an English teacher who had a great deal of class discussion in her lessons, so that of the parts of the lesson which were talk she took up less than half. The extended pupil talk in her lessons is shown in cells 8 – 8 (124 tallies) and 9 – 9 (173 tallies), both of which occur with much higher frequency than average. Her category 5 total (lecture, information giving) is smaller than most others in the sample.[16] There is a much higher incidence of category 1 (acceptance of feeling) than is usually the

79

case, as one element of some of her lessons was discussion of children's emotional reactions to their own or others' writing.

Teacher B was a geography specialist who taught quite differently. Her primary strategy was to give short pieces of information, often supplemented with illustrations and pictorial material, followed by a relatively closed question inviting a fairly predictable answer or set of answers. She would usually accept the answer, clarify perhaps in some way, and then give a further piece of information. This basic pattern $5 - 5 - 4 - 8 - 3 - 5 - 5 - 4 - 8 - 3$ was frequently repeated, and it closely resembled programmed instruction.

It would, of course, be quite wrong to make inferences about the *quality* of the two students' teaching on the basis of Flanders data alone, and observers would have tended to disagree about their relative effectiveness. The main value of interaction analysis data is that students can look at this kind of evidence in the light of all the other cues available to them and then make decisions about future procedures.

Limitations of the Flanders system

The Flanders system is most easily applied in formal classrooms where the teacher addresses the whole class, a pattern more commonly detected in secondary schools than in primary, and most frequently seen in subjects like history and geography. It is much less appropriate in situations where children work in groups, where there is little talk, or where classroom organisation in some other way reduces the observer's ability to hear what a teacher is saying.

Some of the categories are too broad, and other systems attempt to subdivide them. A category like 'praise', for example, fails to distinguish between cursory praise and sincere praise. Category 4 (questions) covers a wide variety of questions, so that Amidon and Hunter[17] used a subdivision into 'broad' and 'narrow' questions, ie those offering a wide and a restricted set of answering possibilities. Category 5 (lecture) makes no differentiation between factually accurate and inaccurate information from the teacher, a crucial issue, or between delivery in a pleasing stimulating manner and that in a dull bornig tone. Rosenshine[18] classifies observational systems as containing either *low inference* measures, ie those where the focus is on specific acts of behaviour, requiring the observer to make little use of subjective judgment, and *high inference* measures, where the observer does have to be subjective. Category 5 as it stands is a *low inference* measure, but if one added the congruent dimension of boring/interesting quality of lecture it would become a high-inference measure. Galloway[19] has designed a set of non-verbal categories such as 'responsive/ unresponsive class' to parallel the Flanders system.

Those who felt that Flanders' two categories of pupil talk were inadequate have created systems that amplify them. Ober,[20] for example, devised a reciprocal category system where all the teacher categories can also be used to describe the behaviour of children. Similarly Hough[21] has subdivided category 10 (silence, confusion) into four separate elements in his 16-category system, those being (a) directed practice or activity, ie non-verbal behaviour resulting from the teacher setting the children to work, (b) silence, (c) demonstration, eg the teacher writes on the board or shows a film, (d) irrelevant behaviour such as noise or confusion.

Since there are so many other systems in existence, some of those suitable for trainee teachers will be described below. First, however, there will be a consideration of the practical issues involved in training students, using pairs of teachers during teaching practice, and the use of interaction analysis as a supervisory tool. References throughout this section will be to the Flanders system, though clearly procedures could be modified according to the system being used.

APPLICATION OF INTERACTION ANALYSIS

Training students

The writer's own experience has been with well over 100 graduate student teachers over a period of five years. During this period groups of volunteers have been trained to use the Flanders and related systems during their three-month teaching practice assignment.

81

The amount of time needed to train students varies according to the degree of observer agreement required. If one assumes that a Scott coefficient of 0.7 is sufficient for student teachers (rather than the 0.8 or 0.85 one might expect for research purposes), training need not be too lengthy and can be completed in four or five 2-hour sessions, which might work out roughly as follows.

Session 1 A group of students is introduced to classroom observation in a general way. They may possibly view a videotape of a lesson if one is available, and attempt to quantify certain aspects of the lesson in their own way, eg looking at the questions the teacher asks, considering the teacher's response to pupils' answers, observing non-verbal aspects such as smiles, movement, materials etc. One possibility is for each trainee to nominate which aspect of the lesson he wishes to study, with suggestions from the tutor if any student feels unable to do this. The advantage of this initial stage is that by analysing some aspect of teaching, however crudely and ineffectively, the student is likely to become curious about other students' observations, realise that classroom transactions are numerous and complex, and be in a better position to derive advantage from the systematic observation schedule he is later to learn.

This opening session is usually lively and full of interesting insights. It does require that the tutor should have available a suitable videotape of a single lesson, or examples of two teachers whose styles are in contrast to each other. The creation of video-taped materials will be considered in a later chapter, but it can be mentioned at this stage that one usually effective way of making videotapes suitable for this session is to give a number of students the same assignment with similar classes or subgroups of classes, and videotape them at work. For example, one could assume that the group of children was going to study pollution over the next few weeks and each student had 10–15 minutes to introduce the topic as interestingly as he could. If the students do this independently of each other, quite a variety of tactics will emerge. The tutor can choose two examples which show very different approaches and use these as material for this first session. Alternatively, if it is felt that the particular group of students would be unwilling to analyse the teaching of their own fellows at this stage, videotapes of teachers or students unknown to the group can be used.

Session 2   Students are introduced to the Flanders system or whatever they are to learn. They should become familiar with the categories and can perhaps look at typescripts of lessons so that ground rules and difficult decisions can be discussed.

This session can include an attempt to code a sound tape of a lesson. It has been the writer's experience that sound tapes of 'real' lessons are rarely clear enough or in other ways totally suitable for training purposes. It is more effective at this stage to create one's own tapes quite artificially. For example, a male tutor and say two or three female students can role-play a 5 or 10 minute imaginary lesson. Although the resulting tape may have a certain air of unreality about it, the advantage of this procedure is that the 'actors' can sit around a microphone, ensuring good quality of sound, and it is usually clear whether it is the 'teacher' or a 'pupil' speaking. An additional bonus comes if all the parties are determined to bring in as many of the categories as they can, when the result is often hilariously funny. It is quite a good activity for the group to make its own simulated lesson.

Once the tape is made, it is advisable not to play too much on the occasion of the group's first attempt at coding. Members of the group should have a clear coding sheet, like the one in Fig 4, to work on, and they can hear the tape a minute at a time. A useful procedure is for the tutor to play the first minute of the tape, stopping it when necessary to discuss categories, difficulties etc, and then to rewind and play the whole minute again. The tutor can help the group develop a sense of the Flanders 3-second time unit by tapping on a table every three seconds as a signal to the student that he should enter a number. On the data sheet one line is filled every minute. By repeating this procedure for, say, five one-minute extracts of the taped 'lesson', the tutor can produce quite a high level of tallying skill even in as little as half an hour. Students should be asked to memorise the categories before the next session.

SCHOOL_____   STUDENT_____
CLASS_____   SUBJECT_____
DATE_____   OBSERVER_____
LESSON (1st 2nd etc)_____

TALLY ACROSS

01																					
02																					
03																					
04																					
05																					
06																					
07																					
08																					
09																					
10																					
11																					
12																					
13																					
14																					
15																					
16																					
17																					
18																					
19																					
20																					
21																					
22																					
23																					
24																					
25																					
26																					
27																					
28																					
29																					
30																					

Fig 4 Lesson observation sheet for up to 30 minutes of classroom interaction

Session 3 By now all members of the group should know the categories and be able to make their decisions without reference to the schedule. In this session they can practise on longer taped lessons, possibly 5 minute sections of a 15 minute tape, with pauses for analysis and discussion. The session can end with a formal reliability check. All members of the group can watch a 15-minute videotape or listen to a sound tape, and category totals can be compared. The tutor may highlight categories which show the greatest incidence of disagreement among students, and the tape can be replayed for discussion and further analysis. In this session students can learn to tally a matrix or apply such other procedures as are involved.

Session 4 The purpose of this session is to introduce students to live observation in classrooms. Students go in groups of four to the classrooms of teachers who have agreed to be observed. They should attempt to code 15 minutes, starting and finishing together, with one member acting as timekeeper and signalling to the others when to start and finish. They then need to withdraw to compare their analyses. After a period of discussion, they should return for a final 15-minute observation, which should by now produce fairly high agreement between them.

Session 5 This takes place back at the college and is the last opportunity for the students to compare experiences, discuss difficulties and possibily code one more 10 or 15 minute tape. Although reasonably high agreement is quite important, it would be a pity to destroy enthusiasm by insisting on unrealistically high agreement and demoralising the group if they have not achieved it. Sources of disagreement are important talking points, and unless the disagreements are profound ones, it is probably as well to go ahead and use the system. Students can still learn a great deal about their teaching as long as disagreements over assignments to categories is not so great as to invalidate the data they collect.

On teaching practice

The supervisor There are several possible applications of inter-action analysis techniques during teaching practice. Used with

85

caution, it can be applied by a supervising tutor or teacher to provide an extra source of information for the student. Caution is needed because it can become a too powerful supervisory tool, enabling the supervisor not only to dictate to students about teaching patterns he sees as desirable, but even to measure with some exactitude whether or not subsequent lessons measure up to his paragon profile. For example, some supervisors have used the technique first of all to demonstrate to the student that he makes criticisms of children (category 7), and secondly that this category should disappear. This is a dangerous procedure, for interaction analysis data should serve as a basis for discussion. It may well be that the supervisor's instincts and experience lead him to conclude that the student is over-critical or harsh in his manner, and that he should do his best to control these tendencies, but the supervisor cannot legitimately suggest that certain categories are bad and ought not to exist.

A second caveat concerns *when* to apply the technique. When classes are in chaos or other pressing problems face the student, interaction analysis data may be of little or no help. The supervisor will also have to sense from other factors, such as the student's personality, the stage of teaching practice, the kind of school and the sort of lesson being observed, whether or not to apply systematic analysis techniques. A number of American studies have investigated the influence of personality on behaviour change in an attempt to discover who is likely or unlikely to change his behaviour as a result of systemic feedback. Zahn,[22] for example, used the Rokeach Scale of Dogmatism to measure open- and closed-mindedness, and one of his findings was that more closed-minded students did show more positive attitudes to teaching after training in interaction analysis, possibly because of the structure it offered.

If interaction analysis is seen by the supervisor to be a useful addition to his normal repertoire of appraisal techniques, and if he feels a particular student understands the system well enough and is sufficiently receptive to gain insights into his teaching from seeing the data, he should be encouraged to use the technique when he feels it to be appropriate. At its best it can be a starting point for profitable and incisive analysis of teaching behaviour.

The student One obvious application of the technique is for students to work singly, in pairs or even in larger groups to analyse their own teaching. A single student who has learned analysis techniques can tape-record his lessons and analyse them himself at his leisure, though it is often difficult to pick up speech clearly on tape, especially when the teacher is mobile or when classroom acoustics are poor. A reasonable quality of recording can often be achieved if the tape recorder is placed near the teacher's desk with the microphone turned towards him and resting on a soft base to cut down background noise. Ideally a radio microphone around the teacher's neck will give excellent quality, provided that financial, technical and bureaucratic obstacles can be overcome.

Pairs of students can quite easily work together to analyse their lessons. It often happens that several students are on school practice together, and that some are free while the others are teaching. One student can sit in on another's lessons and collect data, and on a subsequent occasion they can reverse roles. Similarly a group of three or four students could hold regular teaching analysis sessions, if necessary without either their supervisor or an experienced teacher being present, though both students and supervisors might wish some of the sessions to be attended by both parties. The writer has found it best to use volunteer pairs and groups of students, as assigned pairs will not necessarily work together harmoniously. Assuming a long teaching practice in the middle term of a three term year, a possible programme might emerge as follows:

November/December Volunteers invited to learn interaction analysis system as described above. Trained for four or five sessions. Teaching practice placings should ensure that pairs or groups can operate where possible. Alternatively, if teaching practice placing occurs earlier than November, students can volunteer knowing which pairs or group they will belong to.

January/February/March Students observe each other on teaching practice, possibly every 2 weeks on four or five occasions in all. It is important not to make the task too burdensome, as students have many other priorities and pressures during their teaching practice; on the other hand, it does need to be a regular event if any learning is to take place. If the students observe each other on the same day with the same group once every 2 weeks, there are many possibilities for fruitful discussion and action. One important task for the tutor is to send reminders and notes to students about 3 days before an observation is due. Without these reminders some pairs will fail to make an observation and possibly lose some of their interest as the term progresses and other priorities present themselves. It has been the writer's experience that letters to the students ensure that most complete a schedule of observations and derive a great deal of benefit from them.

At the beginning of the teaching practice students need to be reminded of the procedures. After the Christmas vacation they may have forgotten some important aspect of what had been agreed before the end of the previous term. An example of such a first letter sent to a group of students on teaching practice in secondary schools is given below.

INTERACTION ANALYSIS – PROCEDURES

Here is a list of things to remember when making your observations.

1 Give the class a few minutes to settle down before you start recording. Then record steadily at about twenty tallies per minute, ie one every 3 seconds, until you have recorded a *maximum of 30 minutes*. Try not to get less than *20 minutes*.

2 Sit at the back of the room if possible and try to be discreet.

3 Record fairly and accurately; there are no 'good' or 'bad' lessons as far as the recording system is concerned, so just record what you hear.

4 If in doubt about two categories, eg should this be a 3 or a 5 use the category *farthest away from 5* (but not category 10).

5 At the end of the lesson transfer your data on to the matrix sheet, making sure you have a 10 at the beginning and end of the sequence.

6 *MOST IMPORTANT* – MAKE SURE THAT YOU FILL IN THE TOP OF BOTH THE RECORDING SHEET AND THE MATRIX SHEET, TO SHOW WHO IS OBSERVING, WHO IS BEING OBSERVED ETC.

88

7 *ALSO VERY IMPORTANT* – WRITE ON THE *BACK* OF
THE RECORDING SHEET A BRIEF ACCOUNT OF THE
LESSON, MENTIONING THE SUBJECT BEING
TAUGHT, THE COURSE OF THE LESSON ETC.

WHEN AND WHOM TO OBSERVE

1 Usually you will be observing another student who is on
teaching practice at the same school as you. Sometimes you
may be working as a pair, both observing and being observed.
If there is no student from the college in your school, observe
either a student from another college or a teacher in the school.

2 If you observe a teacher in the school, or a student from elsewhere for that matter, make sure he or she gives you permission
first and KNOWS PRECISELY WHAT YOU ARE DOING.
Most teachers will, I think, cooperate, though not without
some apprehension.

3 *IMPORTANT* – Take *FIVE* observations at approximately
fortnightly intervals.

4 Try to make it the *same lesson on the same day of the week
each time*, eg 3A Geography – Period five – every second
Wednesday.

5 Try to choose a midweek day, rather than Monday or Friday,
and try to choose a class aged between twelve and fifteen. If
you ever miss an observation, try to observe the *same class as
soon afterwards as possible*.

6 Try to get your five observations as near to the following five
Wednesdays as you can: 22 JANUARY, 5 FEBRUARY, 19
FEBRUARY, 5 MARCH, 19 MARCH. Letters of reminder
will be sent to you during the term.

7 Remember that your analysis of the lessons and discussions
about teaching strategies with your fellow observers is a most
important part of the exercise.

From this letter it can be seen that students are encouraged to do
some analysis of teaching even if it is of another student or an
experienced teacher.

An example of the kind of letter which might be sent later in the
term is given below. Clearly a tutor would need to write in the light
of his own students' needs and experiences up to that time.

89

You should try to make your second observation as near to
WEDNESDAY 5 FEBRUARY as you can, preferably with the
same class you observed last time.

On this occasion think about *controlling* your own teaching in the
light of what you discovered from your first observation. For
example, you may have felt you talked too much or too little, or
you may have had certain feelings about the questions you asked.
Were they clear? Did they produce long or short answers or none
at all? How do you use praise and criticism? Again let me remind
you that there are no 'right' answers, you have to make your own
decisions in the light of your own objectives.

When you have made your second observation, you have some
means of comparison. Here are some things you might do to
compare your two lessons. First of all compute percentage totals
for each category as in the example below:

Category	1	2	3	4	5	6	7	8	9	10	Total per cent
1st lesson	0	3	6	11	42	5	3	15	5	10	100%
2nd lesson	1	5	8	16	20	5	5	15	15	10	100%

Some points to consider

1 *How much of the lessons was talk?* 90 per cent in both cases.
2 *How much of the talk was by the pupils?* ie how much 8 and 9
out of categories 1 to 9 inclusive? In the first lesson 20 out of
90, about 22 per cent, in the second less 30 out of 90, about 33
per cent.
3 *How much of the pupil's talk was spontaneous and how much
elicited by me?* ie the proportion of 9 to 8. In the first lesson
pupil talk was a quarter spontaneous and three-quarters
elicited. In the second lesson it was half and half.
4 *What changes have occurred?* In the second lesson the teacher
appears to have talked less, elicited the same amount of pupil
answering, but created more opportunities for spontaneous
pupil contributions; he spent less time giving information
(cat 5), but more asking questions (4), accepting ideas and

90

feelings (3 and 1), and praising and criticising (2 and 7). Commands (6) and Silence etc (10) remain the same.

5 *Is the second lesson better?* It might be, but it might be worse. On this evidence one can only say it is *quantitatively* different. However, if the teacher *meant* to do the things noted, it is possible to say that he is now controlling his own teaching to a certain extent. If his eyes and ears also tell him that the lesson *seemed* better, then he might indeed be becoming a better teacher by controlling his own behaviour and that of the class more effectively.

Your next observation will be on Wednesday 19 February, and I shall write and remind you again just before then. Incidentally if for any reason you didn't make a first observation, start now. Any number of observations are possible, one every two weeks has just been found to be fairly convenient.

One further point needs to be made about the ease of applying a system. Matrix tabulation for the Flanders system is lengthy but often worthwhile. Flanders has described alternative techniques, such as time-line displays, where squares of graph paper can be shaded with a felt-tipped pen every three seconds instead of numbers being written down. This of course fails to preserve *sequence* but does display *amounts* of events. Alternatively, if matrix compilation is felt to be too long, students can simply calculate category totals and look at their lesson observation sheet to see what predominant patterns emerge. This often reveals more than the matrix, as it is possible to pick out strings of four, five or six tallies, such as 5 – 5 – 4 – 8 – 3 or 4 – 8 – 7 – 4 – 8 – 7, which are of considerable interest. It is important that students should feel that lesson analysis is useful and enlightening rather than an irksome chore, so that efforts by the tutor to minimise the mechanical computing element will usually be welcomed. Ideally one would have access to a ten-digit push-button device like a touch telephone, such as designed by Smidchens and Roth,[23] enabling the observer to code directly into a computer which produces a completed 10×10 matrix instantaneously as soon as the lesson is over. At the present, however, this is not likely to be a widely available facility.

91

DIRECTIONS OF CHANGE

So far it has been suggested that the prime use of interaction analysis is to give the student some relatively objective evidence about his teaching in order that he may, taking account of all the other evidence about his teaching available to him, decide on his future action. It has also been argued that as no commonly agreed 'good' teaching patterns have been shown to have universal acceptance, students should not be pressed into prefabricated moulds. There is a possibility, however, that this argument could merely lead to the student groping for elusive styles which he hopes will suit him better than what he might otherwise instinctively settle for. Thus a tutor or supervising teacher using the technique needs to ask himself what his role should be when analysing classroom observation data with students.

Several striking phenomena are commonly observed in students' lessons. Initially the observer is often struck by the stereotype of a teacher as information-giver, which many students have. 'Children need to learn, the teacher knows, the teacher must tell what he knows', runs the argument. With interaction analysis data this role is often highlighted, especially during the early parts of a student's teaching practice. The supervisor should not ask whether this is a good or a bad tactic for a teacher to use, as this would depend on the answers to a vast number of concomitant questions, but rather press the issue of what other roles are available, and whether the student is prepared to explore these.

A further observation is that a number of students never try certain kinds of behaviour. A good example of this occurs in the total absence of categories 2 (praise) or 7 (criticism) from some students' classroom transactions. If one takes the issue of praise, for example, the question is again not whether a student should be urged to use a great deal of it, but if he is aware that he never praises and if this accords with his intentions. It may well be the case that a student never uses praise because he rejects it as a teaching tactic. On the other hand he may frequently fail to use it because he has not stopped to consider its effects as a reinforcer and a possible mode of control. If, with a group of students or an individual, the tutor chooses to highlight the incidence of praise in students' lessons, a lively discussion covering teacher-pupil relations, behaviourist learning theory, the concepts of authority and control and other issues will often ensue.

One of the most exciting possibilities of all is the opportunity for the student to feel that he is a real innovator. The tutor may observe that certain kinds of behaviour rarely or never occur and the student may see this as a challenge to explore what would happen if they did. Some of the writer's own students were one year discussing their teaching in modern language lessons based on data collected by a 20 category system.[24] One striking feature of most lessons was the absence of category 19 (spontaneous pupil talk in the foreign language). The point was made that children's willingness to speak the foreign language spontaneously in class, not merely when asked a question by the teacher, might be not only a good skill for them to acquire, but possibly also one mark of a competent language teacher. Most of the group decided that it would be a challenge to see if they could gradually increase the amount of spontaneous talk in the foreign language in their lessons, and several tried to engineer this by ingenious methods that varied from equipping the class with elementary survival vocabulary in the foreign language ('How do you say —?', 'I don't understand what he just said') to elaborate language games and small group activity. For students with only 5–6 weeks of teaching experience behind them this was an experience which gave them a real taste of the excitement of taking initiatives and attempting to innovate.

Interaction analysis may also have applications outside teaching practice. If our teaching personalities are extensions or projections of what we are normally like as people, a great deal of exploratory work can be done away from the classroom in role-playing exercises (as will be discussed in Chapter 5) or with groups of children brought into the college specially (as will be mentioned in Chapter 4). There will also be an analysis of how videotapes of teachers can be assembled to show different teaching styles.

Finally it should be pointed out that the techniques of interaction analysis do not merely have application possibilities at the initial training stage. Experienced teachers can gain considerable insights into their own teaching even after many years in the classroom.

SOME RESEARCH FINDINGS

The majority of research using interaction analysis with student teachers has taken place in the United States. There are too many studies to mention here but some are of particular interest.

Hough and Amidon[25] found that a group trained in Flanders' interaction analysis technique became more empathic in their relations with children, more experimental and more objective. This research was poorly conducted, with a loose design, so that it is very difficult to say whether the findings are a consequence of interaction analysis training or extraneous variables.

Kirk[26] trained a group of student teachers preparing to teach in elementary schools in the Flanders system and then observed this group and a matched but untrained group on teaching practice. He found that for all students the amount of teacher talk declined over the teaching practice period, but the experimental group elicited more spontaneous children's contributions, engaged in more open discussions and spent less time in continuous lecture. Kirk denies having pointed the experimental group in any particular direction when training them, but admits having made them aware of previous research findings. Presumably this would effectively point them in the direction of greater indirectness and persuade them to elicit more child talk.

Zahn[27] took ninety-two student teachers preparing to teach in elementary schools and gave training in the Flanders system to one quarter of them (n = 23) chosen at random. The group which had been trained showed more positive attitudes to teaching after teaching practice on a pencil and paper test than the others.

Furst[28] took matched groups of student teachers preparing to teach in secondary schools. She gave one group training in inter-action analysis *before* teaching practice, one group training *during* teaching practice, and a third parallel group no training at all. She found that the trained groups showed more acceptance of children's ideas than the untrained group, and that those trained *during* teaching practice produced more children's talk.

94

Moskowitz[29] reported an experiment where the supervising teachers in the teaching practice schools were included. She took forty-four student teachers and the forty-four cooperating teachers who were to supervise their teaching practice, and arranged them at random into four groups. Group 1 was for students and teachers who were both going to be trained to use the Flanders system, group 2 would have students trained but teachers untrained, group 3 would have teachers trained but not the students, and group 4 would have students and teachers both untrained. She administered questionnaires to all eighty-eight participants to measure the positiveness of their attitudes to each other. She also recorded observations of all eighty-eight of them in their classrooms. She concluded that relations between students and cooperating teachers were best in group 1, where both had been trained in the system. In group 2 she detected that the attitudes of students to cooperating teachers were not so good (this was the group in which students were trained but teachers untrained). Groups 1 and 2 (students trained) showed significantly more indirect teaching than groups 3 and 4 (students untrained).

Gunnison[30] took ten student teachers whose teaching style had been observed, using Flanders' technique, to be primarily direct. Half the sample, randomly selected, was given a six-hour course in interaction analysis. The control group received no such instruction. Subsequent observation of all the group showed significantly increased extended indirect influence by the experimental group and significantly greater amounts of pupil talk in the same group. The experimental group was also rated higher by the children. As in many other similar pieces of research there is no control for Hawthorn effect in this experiment. The sample is also too small for very much significance to be inferred from the findings. In addition analysis of Gunnison's data shows a significant rise in the i/d ratio of the *control* group, which she does not explain.

In the field of in-service training Storlie[31] took a group of fifty-one teachers who were undergoing such training and taught them the Flanders system. On the basis of observation data collected on the teachers before they had begun the course he divided them into two groups, one for those who had been seen to be direct and the other for the more indirect. They were then taught by an instructor who adopted either an indirect or a direct teaching style. Most of the teachers in both groups rated the indirect style as more useful and enjoyable.

Withall and Fagan[32] used an interaction analysis technique to classify teacher-centred and learner-centred statements used by teachers before and after a six-week in-service course for teachers of English and reading to disadvantaged children. Analysis of tapes and live observation data showed no change in predominant verbal style in the group of teachers who had undergone the course. There had been, however, a significant impact on the materials the teachers used. Analysis of this aspect showed that teachers made significantly greater use of teacher-prepared materials, showed more contemporary films, used more tapes and audio-visual aids, and individualised their teaching of reading more than they had done before.

The writers conclude that on the evidence of their study much in-service work of the usual kind is likely to make some changes in the variety and type of materials teachers will use, but may make little or no impact on the general teaching style the teacher customarily adopts.

It does seem that, in most of the studies, interaction analysis feedback did have some effect in changing behaviour, but the studies described above failed to make post-training observations over a long term, so these changes may be temporary, merely to please a supervisor who has indicated desirable directions for change.

Three studies have described teaching practice behaviour *without* any kind of interaction analysis feedback. Morgan[33] studied thirty-four students at the beginning and end of their teaching practice period and found no significant difference in the distribution of talk over the ten Flanders categories when he compared first observations with final ones. Schueler, Gold and Mitzel[34] used filmed records of fifty-four student teachers and found more information in what the teacher said, greater class order and greater awareness of children's difficulties at the end of teaching practice. The Exeter enquiry[35] showed greater use of project-type lessons at the end of teaching practice, with a reduction in teacher lecture.

OTHER SYSTEMS

It is not essential for students to learn one of the established systems. As suggested above, they can either design their own observation schedule, or play the role of anthropologist[36] or visiting Martian and pretend they have never in their lives been in a classroom.

If an established and field-tested system is required, there are many to choose from. Careful selection is necessary to ensure that the system chosen best suits the situation, formal or informal, in which the student will find himself. Often it is possible to adapt an existing system in some simple way and make it more appropriate for the student than it was in its original form.

Many of the systems published have been used in research projects and are far too complex for students to learn in a short series of training sessions. Others need elaborate data collection devices or lengthy computer analysis. Yet others are wedded to a particular psychological or philosophical theory, and may not appeal to some students.

Below are some of the more frequently reported systems, grouped according to whether they are *general* systems, capable of being applied in a wide variety of situations, or have a *specific* focus such as the individual child, science lessons or individualised learning. As new systems are being devised and applied all the time, the list is not meant to be exhaustive. Almost all the systems in this section can be found in the Simon and Boyer collection.[37]

GENERAL SYSTEMS

Amidon Modified Category System[38] Takes categories from Flanders, Taba, Hughes and Aschner-Gallagher systems, though basically a modified Flanders system. Subdivides questions into cognitive memory, convergent, divergent and evaluative. Also elaborates on Flanders' praise, criticism and lecture categories.

Amidon and Hunter VICS[39] Another modification of Flanders which elaborates on some of the categories. More variety for pupil talk and has 'teacher rejects' categories.

Aschner-Gallagher[40] Based on Guilford's theories of the intellect and therefore especially useful for analysing the thinking underlying children's talk. Too elaborate for most training purposes with novice teachers, though capable of modification.

Honigman's Multidimensional Analysis of Classroom Interaction[41] Uses sets of symbols, some of which are based on Flanders. The focus is much more on children's talk, however, and the system is simpler to use than many of the modifications.

Hough[42] A modification of Flanders but one based on behaviourist learning theory, containing categories such as 'corrective feedback'. Simple to use if one accepts the underlying theory.

Medley and Mitzel Oscar 4V[43] One of the oldest systems but still a most attractive one. Enables the observer to code pupil to pupil talk as well as teacher-pupil interaction. Divides classroom discourse into 'interchanges' and 'monologues'.

Taba[44] Hilda Taba died just as her work on levels of thought was beginning to show interesting findings. She postulated seven thought levels ranging from 0, 'Incorrect information', up to 6, 'Generalisation from inferences'. Social studies teachers learned, by using the system, how to help children, even those of limited intelligence, to move on to higher levels of thought. Even if one disagrees with her concept of thought levels, there are still intriguing possibilities, and it is to be hoped her work will not be overlooked.

Adams-Biddle[45] Complex to use but of special interest, possibily in a modified form, to those interested in role theory. Explores roles such as 'emitter', 'target', 'auditor', 'disengaged'. Too esoteric perhaps for all but the more avid sociology specialists, but some would learn a great deal from applying it.

Barnes[46] A British system designed for use in secondary schools which examines the teacher's use of questions, whether these be factual, reasoning, open or social. Used with considerable success to enable experienced teachers to analyse their own teaching but would be equally illuminating for beginners.

98

Teacher Practices Observation Record[47] Brown's system is fairly elaborate but has an interesting focus on what Dewey called 'experimentalism'. Especially useful as a measure of how the student's practices in a lesson coincide with his stated beliefs, this system can be used in conjunction with a questionnaire filled in by the student before he is observed.

CERLI (CVC)[48] A simple system developed by the Cooperative Educational Research Laboratory to measure classroom *substance* (what is happening) and classroom *process* (how it is occurring). Easily learned by students, and, moreover, easy to adapt to their own situation if they prefer a home-made system.

Teacher Verbal-non-verbal Coding Instrument[49] Based on some of the objectives from Bloom's Taxonomy. Looks at method (closed and open), objectives (affective and cognitive), and expressions (verbal and non-verbal). Specially designed for ease of administration for teachers to appraise their own classroom behaviour.

SYSTEMS WITH A SPECIFIED FOCUS

Occasionally no satisfactory observation schedule can be found in the systems designed for general use. If a particular teaching subject is to be observed, for example, many general systems will be inappropriate. Several techniques for various subjects have been devised.

Science observation system[50] Altman's aim was to design an easy system which would describe directed and non-directed activity in laboratories, as well as the level of abstraction of classroom discourse. Procedure items, such as classroom management and control, are provided as well as both cognitive and affective categories.

Science Curriculum Assessment System[51] A very usable two-part system for science lessons. The teacher observation schedule has elements for interactions with whole class or smaller subgroups. For observing children the system concentrates on one child at a time for three minutes, gradually building up a picture of the whole class.

99

Biology Teacher Behaviour Inventory[52] Looks at the teacher only and has both verbal and non-verbal dimensions. Difficult to apply for training purposes, though it could be modified. It is certainly a far less complex Biology system than that of Parakh.[53]

Wright-Proctor (*Maths*)[54] A complex system which could only be understood by mathematicians. Would almost certainly need simplifying for use with student teachers, but could be used as a starting point for creating a more straightforward schedule.

FLINT (*languages*)[55] Moskowitz has modified Flanders and assumed that interaction is normally in the foreign language. The postscript E is used when the native language is being employed.

Wragg (*languages*)[56] Another Flanders modification, this time a 20 category system which produces a 20×20 cell matrix. Categories 11 to 20 are the same as Flanders 1 to 10 but are used when interactions occur in the foreign language.

Grittner (*languages*)[57] A useful foreign language system which owes its techniques to Flanders but is less like Flanders than the other two systems cited.

Clements (*Art*)[58] Analyses the questions an art teacher is likely to ask children when they are at work, including experience, judgement, intent, process recall and rule questions. Rule questions, such as 'What do we say about children who don't take time with their pictures?' might suggest that there is a set of rules which children ought to learn in art, and this may appal many art students. It may spur someone to create an alternative observation schedule.

SYSTEMS WHICH FOCUS ON THE INDIVIDUAL CHILD AND ON YOUNG CHILDREN

IPI Student Observation Form[59] Lindvall's system looks at the child working on his own, reading, viewing a filmstrip, using programmed material, waiting to see the teacher or asking another pupil for help. There are group activity categories, too, but the prime focus is on an individual child. This system, possibly with

100

minor modifications, is very suitable for open plan or informal primary schools.

Student Activity Profile[60] Similar to Lindvall's system but enabling the observer to go round a class of children very quickly as he merely codes the first unambiguous behaviour observed for each child and then passes on to another member of the class. Again very suitable for open plan and primary schools.

Kowatrakul[61] Similar to the Student Activity Profile above, in that it enables the observer to code a whole class rapidly. There are six categories of child behaviour and three classroom activities (independent seat work, watching and listening, discussing). Not as good as the two systems above but has some possible merit for informal classrooms.

Evans-Wragg[62] A method of subscripting Flanders-type data to show individual interactions. Longer time needed to build up data for a whole class, but the chief merit is that the student would not need to learn another system if he already knew Flanders. Suitable for any type of informal classroom including schools for subnormal or severely subnormal children.

Anderson[63] First developed in 1939 to study kindergarten children, but still a very usable descriptive tool. Although its original focus was on 'dominative' and 'integrative' acts by the teacher, it can easily be modified so that profiles of individual children's acts can be assembled.

Spaulding (CASES)[64] Specially designed to enable the observer to study young children. Contains categories such as 'aggressive behaviour', 'manipulating others', 'paying rapt attention' and 'physical withdrawal or avoidance'. Could be used in conjunction with the Anderson system or as a basis for a home-made system for observing nursery-age or infants' school children.

Teacher-child Dyadic Interaction[65] Good and Brophy designed this system to enable them to study the relation between teachers' perceptions of their pupils and how they dealt with them in class. It could equally well be used by students in primary schools, as many of the categories, such as 'response opportunities', 'level of question', 'child's answer', and 'work-related, procedural and behavioural teacher-pupil contacts', are very appropriate.

101

One final system is worthy of note and that is Herbert's *System for Analysing Lessons*.[66] This is an elaborate schedule containing too many categories for most purposes but it can easily be broken down into smaller sets some of which, such as 'lesson form', 'media' or 'grouping and location', have several excellent ideas. It would be quite possible, for example, if one's main interest were in the student's use of media, to employ these categories only.

For notes to this chapter see pp 204–8.

4 Micro-teaching

Micro-teaching is normally understood to be a recent development in the training of teachers, requiring extremely expensive television equipment and supervisor's time, and hence out of reach of all but the most generously endowed training institutions. It will be argued here, however, that it is not entirely new, can be used with or without a supervising tutor, and need not be prohibitively expensive.

Micro-teaching, as its name suggests, is a scaled-down version of real teaching. Several factors usually confronting the teacher are reduced in size. The number of pupils, for example, can be cut down from thirty or more to as few as five or six, and the unit of time reduced from a day or a whole lesson to perhaps as little as 5 or 10 minutes. For learning purposes the teacher's potential register of competence is developed not in its totality but rather with special reference to one or two isolated elements. The argument in favour of the technique is that it enables a teacher to develop his repertoire of professional skills in an atmosphere congenial to learning, away from the hurly-burly of normal class-room life, and that, especially for the novice, this relatively 'safe' environment is essential for effective learning to take place. Curiously enough, these same elements are quoted by those hostile to micro-teaching, who reject it precisely because it is detached from 'real' classroom life, and because they see teaching competence as a complex set of skills and relations not amenable to segmentation.

It is proposed in this chapter that micro-teaching as a technique has a useful place in certain kinds of teacher training and that the term should be understood to include a wide number of practices involving some or all of the basic scaling-down principles.

THE ELEMENTS OF MICRO-TEACHING

The basic format for micro-teaching programmes was developed at Stanford University[1] from 1963 onwards and has been extensively reported by Allen and Ryan,[2] Borg et al,[3] and Stones and Morris,[4] among others. As understood by most writers on the subject it would comprise the following seven elements:

1 *Preparation* The student prepares a small lesson often in the light of lectuie/discussion/videotaped material to do with some aspect of teaching and learning.
2 *Skills* He attempts to concentrate his attention on a specific skill such as questioning.
3 *Class size* Usually this is far below the group of twenty to thirty-five frequently encountered.
4 *Time unit* Again this is much less than the normal minimum contact time of 30–40 minutes.
5 *Teach lesson* The student teaches what he has prepared to a small group of children.
6 *Feedback* After he has taught he receives feedback, often in videotape form, about his first attempt at teaching the children.
7 *Reteach lesson* In the light of the feedback he has received he has time to replan his approach and also the opportunity to teach a group similar in nature to the first one he encountered.

At its best this way of organising the early teaching experiences of trainee teachers can offer them considerable insights into teaching and even produce a real sense of excitement in both the student and the supervisor (where the latter is also involved). All those involved in micro-teaching have their own memories of the process working well. Two examples from the writer's own experience may illustrate some of the possibilities.

Example 1 Paul, a slightly nervous student always known to be conscientious and well prepared in all he does, who also has a gentle, unforceful and kindly manner, has prepared some material to help initiate a discussion on sea trade. In his first lesson with a small group of ten year olds he reads an extract from *Robinson Crusoe* describing a shipwreck scene, in an attempt to show the children how dangerous life at sea can be. After this he shows pictures of different kinds of ships and tells the children some of the goods normally carried by water. His occasional questions produce cursory replies.

As he watches the videotape of his lesson he makes a number of important discoveries. He sees the bored expressions during his lengthy and badly read extract. He comments on the ineptitude of some of his questions and his tendency to hold up pictures very briefly, not giving everyone a chance to see them. Finally he reads the children's written comments, which confirm that they were not interested and have failed to understand the point of what was going on. He goes away to plan his reteach lesson, resolving (a) to shorten the story extract to a few particularly telling paragraphs which he can read with greater zest, (b) to use the pictures more effectively, (c) to ask more suitable questions.

In the reteach lesson he holds the attention of the class quite well as he reads the particularly dramatic story extract. Immediately he finishes, he asks the question: 'If life at sea can be *so* dangerous, why do people go out in ships?' After a short pause he is offered several explanations, many of which offer a natural lead-in to the pictures he has brought along. The children's written comments afterwards show that they have really enjoyed the lesson, and they make observations such as, 'I never thought about ships that way before', or 'I've never been interested before in why people send things by ship, but I am now.'

Example 2   Helen has, with enormous care, prepared a lesson on volcanoes. She teaches the first lesson by giving the class a number of pieces of information about the nature of volcanoes, more or less as follows: 'Today I want to tell you a little bit about volcanoes. Here is a model of one and you can see that this is the crater and, as you probably know, this is the lava, and this part here is called the magma chamber. Perhaps you've heard of volcanoes before. There's one in Italy called Vesuvius . . .'

When she watches the videotape, she is disappointed by the class's poor response on the rare opportunities she has given them to contribute. Her supervisor suggests she might start off the reteach lesson by simply asking the class what they know about volcanoes and following up from this.

She begins by asking the class what they know about volcanoes. As often happens there is no reply, but she repeats the question and waits. Gradually, after the first few hesitant responses, more and more children contribute, referring to television programmes; their own, their friends' and parents' holiday and travel experiences; and things they have read in books. In the ensuing few minutes various children mention Vesuvius, Etna, Krakatoa, Sertsey, craters on the moon, Icelandic geysers and Tristan da Cunha, some readily using terms such as lava and eruption. Helen is delighted but also taken by surprise both by the breadth and depth of their knowledge.

The two examples cited above show how it is possible for a novice teacher to gain considerable insights into teaching and children's learning and thinking in a relatively short period of time. In both cases the teach and reteach cycle had been completed in around $1\frac{1}{4}$ hours. It would, of course, be erroneous to pretend that all reteach lessons are a huge success and clearly show increased competence, or even that the reteach lessons described above are either typical or demonstrate detectable progress. Some are arguably worse, even catastrophic perhaps, as the student struggles to modify his behaviour too radically or in directions which do not suit him. In general, however, those offering programmes which provide micro-teaching experiences spread over a longer period of time would tend to endorse the claim that they provide substantial opportunities for students to explore and gain insights into various aspects of teaching. It is the cumulative effect which is ultimately of importance.

Examinations of the seven elements catalogued above will reveal that many possibilities are available within the micro-teaching format.

PREPARATION

For the student to gain maximum benefit from his first teaching encounter in the micro-teaching cycle, he needs careful preparation and there are numerous options available. First of all he could receive some formal instruction from a supervisor. For example, if the skill under consideration was reinforcement of children's responses, students might be given a lecture on reinforcement theory by a psychologist. This tends to be rather an arid approach and one contrary to the essential spirit of micro-teaching, which is that the student should feel the practical reality of what he experiences.

It might be better, therefore, if the students studied videotapes of various teachers using different styles of reinforcement, which leads on to the question of modelling considered below. If video-tapes are not available, sound tapes or even lesson transcripts can be almost as useful. Given reasonable sound or videotape-editing facilities, it is quite easy to cull a variety of examples of a skill like reinforcement from existing tapes to show common examples, such as the teacher saying 'Good' or smiling, or more sophisticated ones, as when the teacher uses a child's idea or adopts his suggestion, as well as the token reinforcement which occurs when the teacher repeats 'Good' mechanically and perhaps without any really reinforcing effect.

There should also be an opportunity for the students to discuss a concept like reinforcement from a number of angles before passing on to the next skill. There could be a consideration of psychological theories of reinforcement, the language of reinforcement, the very important non-verbal aspects such as warmth, enthusiasm and other supportive concomitants of overt praise. Many students would want to discuss the philosophical aspects of deliberately using reinforcement techniques, especially as a means of *control*, since reinforcement by the teacher presumably increases the likelihood of the approved behaviour recurring. Similarly, some might want to question whether it should be called a skill at all, and whether they feel they themselves can readily employ it as a deliberately chosen teaching tactic. Whether such options are available for the students depends on the degree of directiveness shown by the supervisor. Some may wish to provide students with experiences of the chosen set of skills and leave them to decide subsequently whether or not they employ them, whereas others may feel easier if students are themselves well disposed and as fully informed as possible before they explore any skill.

Modelling

Learning by imitating experienced practitioners is among the oldest teacher training techniques (see Chapter 1). Early work at Stanford was considerably influenced by Albert Bandura's studies of the effects on social learning of model imitation,[5] including the effects on children of seeing aggressive adults on film. Since that time a number of investigators have explored a variety of modelling procedures. McAleese and Unwin[6] are among writers who have examined the nature of effective models.

Several questions need to be considered before one can best choose the models to which students are exposed. One key point is the degree of association in the student's mind between himself and the model, for there needs to be a relatively high degree of empathy if viewing the model is to be a springboard for action. For example, seeing a dazzlingly proficient teacher might depress rather than encourage the student, suggesting that the gap between the substantial skill he sees on videotape and what he guesses to be his own miserable ineptitude is impossible to bridge. Yet, on the other hand, seeing lessons given by teachers barely more skilful than himself might provide too little learning opportunity.

On balance it seems that there are real advantages to having a variety of videotaped examples available – some by experienced teachers, some showing poor examples as well as good, and others, perhaps role-played, even exaggerating the skill a little. The tutor will need to select the examples with care, for too many might simply overwhelm and paralyse the student. The tutor has an important part to play here in helping students view videotapes with discrimination, though this need not mean the student simply learning to accept the tutor's views about teaching.

The skill of set induction, ie starting off a lesson, could be prepared in a variety of models. The writer used six different models, all enacted by himself, to show different ways of setting up a lesson or series of lessons on 'racial strife'. The students were to imagine that they would be taking a class of thirteen-year-olds for a number of sessions and that their task was to explore the nature of conflict between people of different races. The following six models for the start of the first session were shown.

Model 1 A teacher lecture approach. The teacher delivers a factual lecture along the lines, 'Since the war immigrants from various countries have come to live in Britain. In some towns and cities there are more immigrants than others, as foreign workers here tended to find jobs where there are industries like textiles. On the whole we seem to have avoided the major race riots which other countries have experienced, but that doesn't mean that British people are never prejudiced . . .'

Model 2 Making use of a topical event. The teacher begins: 'You have in front of you a copy of a letter which a Member of Parliament has received from an old lady in his constituency. Let us look through it and try to work out why she has written to her MP . . .' A lively discussion about the issues involved then begins.

Model 3 Gaining a commitment from the class. The teacher says: 'I'm going to ask you some questions and even though you probably don't know the answers, I want you to guess as sensibly as you can.' Questions are then asked about numbers of immigrants, family size and housing. Children write down their guesses and then compare them with recently published figures, both official and those of government critics who offer higher estimates. A discussion follows.

Model 4 Use of musical stimulus and children's experience. Teacher asks: 'Can you tell me any words you know or have heard people use which describe black people?' Class produces a list of several, mainly derogatory. Teacher plays the song 'I'm a coloured spade' from the musical *Hair*, and discussion ensues.

Model 5 Role play and small group activity. Teacher begins: 'I want you to split up into ones and twos. Those in a pair will pretend that they live either side of a man who is selling his house to an immigrant family, and they must plan what they will say to him when they go round to try to persuade him not to sell. Those on their own will pretend they are the man in the middle house and they suspect their neighbours may be upset, so they have to work out how they will justify selling.' The teacher is then shown setting up the ones and twos and helping them. Finally one of the actual role plays is enacted before the class.

Model 6 Open question. Teacher asks: 'What do you under-

109

stand by the word "prejudice" '? He subsequently plays a chairman role as various members of the class offer suggestions, asking occasional supplementary open questions.

These six models are merely some of the infinite number of possibilities available. If the same person is used for all six, as was the case above, it is important that he should not try too hard to 'sell' a particular model at the expense of another. It would be easy, for example, to imply that a lecture type opening is a bad one by delivering a thoroughly boring and possibly even factually inaccurate lecture. Since the differences for the student should be ones of *style*, the lecture approach should be as stimulating as any of the others.

An alternative method of getting a variety of models for a set induction session would be to give a number of teachers the same brief, and to film each of them starting off the class. There would then be a variety of models to choose from, each reflecting the idiosyncracies of a different person. The tutor could choose the most suitable examples for the particular group concerned and his own programme needs. In any case it is advisable to create one's own material for these sessions, for part of the excitement and commitment comes from this original creative exercise. A tutor feels less committed to someone else's materials than his own, and students will derive less benefit if the tutor himself only marginally approves of what he is using.

The final point to be considered under the broad heading 'preparation' is the student's own preparation for his teach lesson in the teach-reteach cycle. It can often be advantageous for pairs or small groups of students to prepare their teach lessons jointly. There are three main reasons for this. First of all many students, especially near the beginning of their training, which is when micro-teaching is most likely to be employed, lack both confidence and the experience of generating good ideas for lessons. In a small group suggestions can often emerge and be developed during group interaction, and this mutually supportive atmosphere can be very helpful to all but the most parasitic. Secondly, the pair or small group can share the critique sessions with similar supportive effects. Thirdly, and of equal importance, especially when the same class of children is regularly used as guinea pigs, there can be some continuity for the pupils. It would be easy to forget that the children need to get something out of the sessions, and a system where they are nothing more than teaching fodder for novices to experiment on is not a healthy example for students. Pairs and small groups of students can ensure that there is some continuity of experience for the children and that they are not merely the recipients of a series of disjointed and conceptually unrelated episodes.

Students should be encouraged to plan even the smallest unit of teaching with great care and circumspection. There is little substance in the argument that if they spend an hour planning a 10 minute 'lesson', they might need to spend 30 hours planning each school day. It is precisely because micro-teaching is an unreal situation that they can afford this luxury. They will learn a great deal about lesson planning at this early stage of their career – for example, that *what* one teaches (the subject matter) is not independent of or worth less consideration than *how* one teaches it (the strategies employed). This last lesson is normally learned by student teachers more expensively, and at the cost of much more nervous stress, during teaching practice itself.

PRIMARY SKILLS

The prerequisite of any micro-teaching programme is a careful analysis of the teaching skills to be systematically explored and developed. This is not a simple task, partly as a result of the chaos which exists in the teacher-effectiveness research literature. Unless one is prepared, however, to try and define the skills of teaching, the micro-teaching programme as it currently exists cannot even be started. It is indeed possible to use the micro-teaching format in a skill-free framework, where students teach and reteach for the benefits that can accrue simply from practice, but some degree of focus is needed if maximum advantage is to be derived.

Allen and Ryan[7] postulated fourteen component skills in the Stanford programme, but these can be reduced to a set of five:

1 *Questioning* – fluency in asking questions; probing, higher-order and divergent questions.
2 *Starting and finishing* – set induction and closure.
3 *Interest and variety* – stimulus variation, illustrating and use of examples.
4 *Communication* – lecturing, completeness of communication, non-verbal cues, planned repetition.
5 *Sensitivity* – recognising attending behaviour, reinforcement of children's participation.

This was an admirable first attempt to create a framework within which the Stanford programme could function, but many institutions adopted the Stanford list of component skills as a standard blueprint instead of a preliminary plan that could be modified or expanded in ways relevant to their own student teachers, and it is in this area that micro-teaching is at present most likely to become arid and institutionalised. Ward's study[8] of 141 US teacher training institutions which used microteaching in their secondary education programme showed that the most popular skills taught, namely asking questions, set induction, reinforcement, use of examples and varying the stimulus, were all on the original Stanford list. They tend to be relatively low inference variables, presumably so that behaviour change can more easily be quantified and monitored by evaluators. Yet the real challenge might lie in exploring high-inference variables such as warmth, enthusiasm, clarity, helpfulness or rapport, despite the snares which the lack of precision of such terms conceal. Even if a tutor's own perspectives lead him to identify sets of skills other than those described above, few would contest their importance.

Questioning

More than any other skill this one lends itself to some of the interaction analysis techniques described in Chapter 3, where several of the systems described not only subdivided questions but also offered means for students to explore a variety of questions and even to attempt to lead a class on to higher levels of thought by shrewd use of questions.

A common distinction needs to be made between the restrictive question, which is often little more than a command to the pupil to vocalise the single word in the teacher's mind, eg 'What is the capital city of France?', or the open question, which offers wider possibilities. 'What, then, is the meaning of life?' is the broadest to come to the writer's attention in recent years.

Higher order questions prove to be among the most elusive for students to frame effectively. Taba's work[9] on levels of thinking in children is relevant here, and students can learn to guide children to what Taba designated higher level thought processes by judicious use of questions. Simple recall, therefore, would be a response to a lower level question, whereas if the teacher required a child to make predictions ('What do you think happened after the army had been defeated?'), inferences ('If the pioneers had to walk long distances, how do you think this affected their lives?') or even generalisations from inferences ('What is the difference between witch doctors' and our doctors' treatment of tropical disease?'), then these would all be questions invoking a higher order of thinking.

Supplementary or probing questions comprise another kind often ignored by trainees who feel sufficient has been achieved by their initial enquiry. The experienced teacher on the other hand will sense partial understanding in the respondent, or an opportunity to delve more deeply into the issue, and press on with perhaps a series of further questions, as in the sequence below:

Teacher: Why doesn't Tony believe the old man?
Helen: Because he thinks he's lying.
Teacher: Why does he think he's lying?
Michael: Because he saw him take the necklace.
Teacher: Did he actually *see* him take the necklace?
Michael: Well, he thought he saw him put something into his pocket.

Equally important in this particular set of skills is not only the teacher's question but his subsequent behaviour, including his reading and handling of the silence which may follow. Many

113

students have such a fear of the silence that they answer themselves, often within 2–3 seconds. Even 5 seconds of silence can seem an eternity to the anxious novice, and in his eagerness to fill the vacuum he signals only too clearly to the class that he seems to prefer his own answers to theirs.

One useful aspect of the skill of questioning, however, is that, more than any other, it can be illustrated by typescript. It is possible to assemble numerous examples of teachers' questions and analyse, rephrase, group or label them. It is also more straightforward to predetermine certain key questions the teacher may wish to use at strategic times if the opportunity presents itself.

Starting and finishing

Set induction, or ways of making an interesting start to a lesson, is not a difficult skill to practice. It is probably the most natural of all the Stanford skills in that the student really is starting off with the group, and the only disappointment is that his time may have expired at the very moment when his opening has worked. Also there is common agreement that the early stages of an encounter in the classroom can be crucial.

Closure is quite different. It is first of all difficult in the usually short period of time available to practise closure, which is a much more complex and subtle series of events than it might at first seem to the beginner. If the spirit of micro-teaching is to isolate skills for intensive analysis and practice, then closure, while amenable to analysis, is much less open to intensive practice, as the student can hardly greet his class with a series of paraphrases of 'In conclusion . . .'

Furthermore closure can be seen as an act of administrative tidiness, suggesting that lessons must be tidied up, with children dismissed after the teacher has summarised what has been learned. Johnson distinguishes between cognitive closure, when children have related new learning to old knowledge, and instructional closure, when the teacher has made this link,[10] and it is frequently important that the link should occur. Yet it is of equal concern for lessons to be seen as a series of learning opportunities, and this is perhaps where micro-teaching is least useful. Many teachers

114

would want to do quite the reverse of packaging their lessons neatly, sometimes preferring to achieve an intriguing sense of incompleteness which can give the following lesson a much more interesting opening. This aspect should not be forgotten when the skill of closure is under scrutiny.

Finally the logistics of starting and finishing should not be overlooked. Teachers need considerable organisational skills to set up and terminate certain kinds of activity. Even though the mechanics of assembling and distributing materials, assigning to groups, explaining the task and clearing away afterwards need not be the prime concern, their inept handling will spoil the best prepared lesson.

Interest and variety

Here are skills which are particularly challenging on the creative ingenuity of teachers, and poor performances with classes can often be traced back to failures to arouse interest or provide variety. Generations of children, including student teachers themselves, can testify to the grinding senseless predictable boredom of lessons given by desiccated husks who appear to have died on the job and been allowed to stay on posthumously, and such experiences are dehumanising both for teacher and taught.

Under stimulus variation one would wish to include not only changes of pupil activity but shifts in teaching style, both verbal and non-verbal. It was described in the previous chapter how limited and predictable the predominant verbal style of student teachers tended to be, ie those who lecture tend to do this regularly, those who produce short pupil responses to closed questions adopt a programmed instruction format and so on. There will be some discussion in the section on feedback below about the use of interaction analysis techniques to apprise students if their own verbal style appears to be very restricted.

Non-verbal variety can be achieved by use of gestures and other bodily movement. Gestures tend to be idiosyncratic and the results of certain emotional needs. Inner stress or other kinds of tension produced by fear or hostility can produce vigorous movement or, alternatively, restrain the teacher like a straitjacket.

115

Moreover children read emotional states as manifested by gestures as clearly as they read simple books. No amount of verbal pyrotechnics by the apprehensive student can conceal or compensate for the drawn expression, the nervous tie adjusting or handbag searching, the downward gaze attempting to avoid eye contact, or the embarrassed hand movements. From the moment he stumbles over an obstacle, writes in an unpractised hand with too long a stick of chalk which squeals and fragments its way across the chalkboard, or searches in anguish for the blackboard cleaner which all, apparently, except he can see, he is marked as a novice, and maybe that is how it should be until he gains confidence.

All this suggests that the highlighting of gestures may be among the most artificial activities, unless one particular mannerism occurs so frequently as to distract the class's attention. One is particularly depressed by the unintentionally skeletal micro-taught smile at the viewers by the commentator on Stanford University's own early film made to popularise micro-teaching. Yet it would be wrong to label analysis and development of gestures and movement as taboo. They certainly are important constituents of variety, and, unless self-consciousness paralyses the student rather than releases him, it is right that they should receive attention. But it would also be wrong to ignore the fact that this area needs sensitive handling by the tutor or supervisor.

What Allen and Ryan call 'shifting sensory channels' (inducing the class to use another form of perception) is excellent material for micro-teaching, especially where subject or audio-visual specialists are available as resources personnel. Here the student has to think very much as if he were a member of the class, sensing the feeling of fatigue which occurs when children only listen to the teacher. He needs to ask himself what they might *look at* (filmstrip, chart, duplicated sheet, blackboard illustration, overhead projector slide, demonstration, mime, role play), *listen to* (music, sounds, teacher's voice, other children, tape, record), *feel* (textures, Cuisenaire rods, science materials, animals, models), and even *taste* and *smell* if appropriate. All these need to be considered separately and in combination, and the student needs to learn when a switch to another kind of sensory input is desirable.

116

Very often the child's only option out of the infinite number of possibilities is the teacher's voice.

Related to this is the use of illustrations and examples. Many students in their early weeks of teaching practice find this most difficult. They have been encouraged to use material which is close to children's experience, yet they cannot know what children's experience comprises until they have spent a period of time in their intimate company. Furthermore they find that, unlike some of the more experienced teachers they see, they are unable to invent suitable examples at short notice in the middle of lessons as the other pressures on them often work to prevent quick thinking. For these reasons micro-teaching offers good opportunities for the student, alone or as a member of a group, to devise suitable examples in advance and use these if they seem appropriate in the lesson.

Communication

All teaching is arguably some kind of communication, but here this heading means the more overt kind of teacher information-giving and direction. The main difficulty with students is not so much their developing teacher lecturing skill as persuading some of them that other strategies are available. As all teachers will at some time wish to communicate information in their own particular way, it is obvious that attention must be paid both to the skill's quality and quantity.

Planning is most important, as the teacher has little excuse if the information he gives is demonstrably inaccurate or of dubious value. Non-verbal aspects such as eye contact are easily forgotten, and many lecturers become note-bound, losing their audience as a result. The student needs to learn to scan his class as he relays the information to see if they appear to be interested, paying attention, listless, bewildered or bursting to interrupt and ask a question. Telling a story to a group of children is a good activity here as the student needs to read with expression, consult his book, yet split his attention between that and the class. More demanding still is to tell a story without a book. One administrative advantage of storytelling in this context is that it can have a certain completeness within the short time normally available.

There are also the skills of planned repetition and timing generally. The student needs to find his own version of the time-honoured tip to information-givers: 'Tell them what you are going to tell them; tell them; tell them what you have told them.' More subtly he needs to learn modifications of the straight lecture technique, such as the seeding of questions with further information ('What did the army do after the battle, and remember what time of year it was?') or the limited effectiveness of masses of information poured out by the teacher when unsupplemented by illustration or class participation. Some of the findings of investigators like Hovland[11] would be useful here. Hovland investigated factors such as the placing of key items of information or pro and contra arguments in a lecture to see what sequences were most effective in changing opinions or forming impressions in the listeners. He found, among other things, that if contradictory points of view were presented, the first one presented tended to dominate in the thoughts of the listeners, and that opinions were changed more readily if communications most desirable to the audience were presented before those less desirable.

As delicate as the question of gestures raised above are the non-verbal aspects of communication – the smiles, facial expressions, nods and other amplification signals which accompany a piece of information-giving. One might include here too the pitch, timbre and volume of the speaker's voice. Several students founder because, despite careful preparation and sound ideas, they are simply inaudible. It is not the place here to describe at length the techniques available to improve this aspect, but notable in passing are works frequently written for actors but suitable for teachers by Horner[12] on movement, voice and speech, especially the transfer of feeling to voice and the achievement of coordinated bodily and vocal expression; Ward[13] on articulation and vocal training generally; Fishman[14] on acting, which has some very useful, and often amusing speech exercises; and the unorthodox but stimulating approach to vocal and acting techniques of Grotowski.[15] Some of these ideas will be discussed again below.

118

Sensitivity

This is not the best blanket term to embrace both awareness of pupils' reactions and reinforcement, but the two can be considered separately.

atMicro-teaching offers good opportunities for students to become tuned to children's needs and reactions. One source of feedback to be discussed below is children's reports on the lesson. Videotapes, especially where one camera has picked up children's reactions, may not only reveal to the student how children are bored, distracted, or fooling about, but show clearly how much the teachers have missed by failing to scan the class because they were too busy trying to teach the children something.

Reinforcement is a different matter. It was stated above that the student should be given an opportunity to examine his own and other students' attitudes to it as a teaching tactic. There is no doubt that all teachers, even those who apparently never use overt praise as a motivating weapon, have techniques of reinforcement. They have signalled that they are pleased or satisfied in some other way. If a teacher always criticises children's answers or efforts, it may be reinforcing on the rare occasions when he makes no response to their work, indicating that he is marginally less dissatisfied than usual. Smiles, nods, physical pats, jokes all represent overt use of reinforcement. Use of children's ideas may be an even more powerful reinforcer.

A large number of investigations have confirmed the powerful conditioning effect of skilfully used reinforcements, particularly on certain types of personality. Amusement arcades crowded with people dourly and obsessively feeding fruit machines with coins, most of which fail to return, testify daily to the controlling effect of random reinforcement.

The labelling of reinforcement as a teaching skill ought not to lure one into pressing students into using it liberally without considerable forethought. There is little doubt that it is a conditioner, that it facilitates certain kinds of learning in many different types of people, or that most teachers use it quite deliberately. It is perhaps too cynical to imply that teachers only use it for control, for often it is the most rational response to genuine pleasure by the teacher, which, as it happens, is also likely to ensure that the child will act in a similar teacher-pleasing way in future.

The tutor should resist the temptation to evaluate the use of reinforcement solely on the basis of the quantity of reinforcing statements or acts noted in the reteach lesson. It is too easy to make teach/reteach comparisons after a lesson in which reinforcement was the issue and satisfy oneself that the occurrence of a greater number of acts of reinforcement means that the objectives of the session have been achieved. It is a much more subtle issue than this.

OTHER SKILLS

It was lamented above that in most institutions the Stanford skills have been adopted uncritically, though since most of the institutions using the technique are at an early stage of development, this is hardly surprising. It would be a great pity for the Stanford skills to become immutably encapsulated. Each institution needs to find its own set of skills, which in most cases might be modifications of the Stanford ones or even the Stanford set as it stands. There are several avenues for exploration and those suggested below are by no means exhaustive.

Subject specific skills

The foreign language teacher needs to sense when to use the foreign and when the native language. He also needs, in an audio-visual lesson, to operate or supervise the use of machines such as tape recorders and projectors, as well as to keep contact with members of the class.

In science lessons the teacher's interaction with a pair of children doing an experiment may be crucial, as may be the question of intervention for safety reasons or to guide pupils towards some discovery rather than tell them what they ought to be finding. Helping a child use a miscroscope may be appropriate for the biologist.

In drama lessons use of space, music, movement, and awareness of children's anxieties are of concern. Much of the content may be individual tuition, as would be the case in hearing a child read or going through an assignment.

All subjects have specific skills attached to them, and although these might usually be subsumed under the general skills described above (for example, all the situations described above may involve reinforcement, questions, stimulus variation etc), it might be better to start from a list of subject specific skills and then amplify these from a list of general skills rather than the other way round. It may be possible to give all students practice in general skills one term and in subject-specific skills later. Alternatively, general and subject-specific skills might be interwoven.

High-inference skills

Some attention should be given to skills which are not so easy to classify because they involve a complexity of subskills, and not so easy to quantify because of the subjective element in assessing them. One could argue that a high-inference variable like 'warmth' or 'enthusiasm' contains identifiable non-verbal elements like smiles, gestures, eye contact and perhaps physical contact, and equally identifiable verbal elements such as learner supportive statements, reinforcement, use of children's ideas or humour. There may be a case for not segmenting these and then hoping the student will reassemble them, but rather for taking the set of behaviours involved as a single group. Despite the difficulties this is worth exploring.

Age-group and school-specific skills

Although teachers in all kinds of schools and at all levels ask questions, give information etc, there are clearly differences in the skills necessary with severely subnormal children, young children, older children, delinquents and highly selected children. These skills may be identified and practised. With younger children there may be much more physical contact than with older ones well aware of touch taboos. With deaf children quite different modes of communication need to be learned. Nor does this point merely apply to extremes. Although skilful teachers can perhaps

121

operate in most situations, part of the difficulty of moving schools is that one needs to learn new skills for the new groups of children one is likely to meet, since each geographical area is unique. Again it is a question of starting points. For some training institutions it might be essential to start with specific skills – training teachers of the blind, for example – but for others the general skills, modified if necessary, may be wholly appropriate.

CLASS SIZE

Stanford used classes of four children who were recruited and paid a dollar a day for their work as guinea-pig pupils. They were fired if they misbehaved,[16] according to best Darwinist principles. They were also taught how to evaluate teachers' performance on the Stanford Teacher Appraisal Scale.

No universally optimum size can be postulated. In certain cases, like the hearing of reading mentioned above, the number might only be one. The trainee scientist might work with a pair of children doing an experiment. For normal purposes four might be adequate, but many people might feel it is too few and eight or ten would be better. There might be a case for increasing numbers gradually, perhaps starting with four and building up to twelve, or even having three standard groups of five, ten and fifteen, with the student working through until he can cope with the fifteen. Certainly size should be kept small, far below normal class sizes, or else part of the value of the experience is lost.

Schools are frequently willing to provide a whole class of children who can be split up into several smaller subgroups. It is important, wherever possible, to ensure that the children are as similar as possible to the pupils normally encountered by students, but as a second best any children might be acceptable.

Rather than dismiss naughty children, it might be as well to allow the student to encounter some early in his experiences. In the short encounter time allowed it is hardly likely they will behave very badly, but most people with experience of micro-teaching report that children are often very quick to settle down in studio conditions, and, especially if they are with their friends, will misbehave quite readily. Since fear of loss of control and poor classroom discipline have been shown in Chapter 2 to be among the student teacher's greatest apprehensions before teaching practice, any indiscipline will provide useful discussion material, as long as he is not becoming demoralised.

The point was made above that the children should get something out of their experience, especially when the same class comes regularly to the studio, and it is often possible to build some of the lessons around a theme planned and executed by a group of students working together. It may be preferable to use the same squad of children so that they become familiar with the procedure, rather than successions of bewildered groups who barely have time to work out what is happening before they are escorted back to school, never to return to the college again.

The final point to be considered is whether or not the children should be trained or primed to do certain things. At Stanford they had to learn certain elementary evaluation procedures, but there are other possibilities. They might learn to role play, ie behave in certain ways allocated to them beforehand, be instructed to be particularly helpful if a student is known to be having his first nervous attempt at teaching, or misbehave so another student can try coping with unruliness. It would be possible to sensitise them to certain aspects of classroom dynamics, even to learn a particular interaction analysis system so that they could consciously manipulate classroom exchanges. The process is fraught with dangers and could become very unreal, but it merits some exploration.

TIME UNIT

Time units of 5, 10, 15 and 20 minutes are all commonly reported by the various institutions using micro-teaching. Some use a 20 minute unit for the student's initial lesson so that this can form the basis for a diagnosis and individual programme. Routine teach and reteach lessons lasted 5 minutes in the original Stanford arrangements. Too little time means the student barely has the chance to begin before being stopped again; too much time can produce a plethora of incidents for analysis and also prove to be too close to normal teaching and therefore not sufficiently scaled down. The issue of time is clearly a matter for individual taste and is open to experiment. The writer has found 10 minutes adequate for most purposes but clearly too short for others, especially when the student needs to set up an activity which involves children working in groups. One option in this latter case is for two students to work together. The first one is responsible for set induction, establishing the groups and ensuring they have understood and begun the task, and the second, who takes over after 15 minutes, can also practise small group and person to person interaction, and is responsible for closure. This gives the children a half-hour and each student 15 minutes; the two students and the supervisor can share planning and critique sessions.

The other concern about time units is with the question of massed and distributed practice. If a student is to experience, for example, two hours of contact with children, there are numerous ways in which this might be distributed, just a tiny number of which are shown below.

1   One 2 hour session
2   Two 1 hour sessions
3   Four 30 minute sessions
4   Six 20 minute sessions
5   Eight 15 minute sessions
6   Twelve 10 minute sessions
7   Twenty-four 5 minute sessions
8   One 20 minute session, eight 10 minute sessions, one 20 minute session
9   Four 5 minute sessions, four 10 minute sessions, four 15 minute sessions
10 Three 5 minute sessions, three 10 minute sessions, three 15 minute sessions, one 30 minute session
11 Six 15 minute sessions and six 5 minute sessions held alternately
12 Six 10 minute sessions, the remaining hour to be apportioned according to needs revealed in the first sessions

Each of these is defensible, some more readily than others. For example (3) is realistic in terms of secondary school lessons; (6) offers twelve separate occasions for practice; (8) gives a diagnostic lesson, plenty of skill practice and a final comparison lesson; (9) and (10) gradually increase the amount of time the student is exposed, and (10) ends with a 'realistic' time unit; (11) gives a chance to practice six skills and a short follow-up opportunity to work at some small aspect of them; (12) offers grounding in basic skills and flexibility for each student to be assigned to subsequent experiences in the light of his manifested needs.

Some of these arrangements are more straightforward administratively than others, but the prime concern is obviously how students best learn. Factors to be considered include personality of student, age-group and subject to be taught, availability of children, technical facilities available, and supervisors' time and preferences. Apart from suggesting that distributed practice probably offers the best opportunities both for student learning and for the integration of theory and practice, as described by Perrott and Duthie[17] at the University of Stirling, it does seem that distribution needs to be arranged in the light of local conditions. For the programme to have any real effect probably a minimum of four sessions is required, but this again depends on the timing of micro-teaching in the student's training experience. Four sessions might be useful before a first teaching practice, but selected students might need to receive several further intensive sessions before subsequent school practices.

TEACH LESSON

As the teach lesson is a first attempt at the skill under consideration, neither student nor supervisor can do more than guess what the outcome will be. It is the payoff after the planning and preparation that has preceded it, and it provides discussion material for the critique session. It is quite possible that the student will experience as many as fifty interpersonal transactions of various kinds in a 10 minute time span. Ideally, once he has recovered from the so-called 'cosmetic effect' of seeing himself in action, he will begin to identify those aspects of his teaching which appear to be developing strengths, and those detectable weaknesses which need special corrective action. This leads on to the very important question of what kinds of feedback are going to provide him with the best opportunity both to learn and to modify his teaching where necessary.

FEEDBACK

Commonly known as KR (knowledge of results) in the research literature, feedback, or the effects of knowing the consequences of behaviour on learning, has been studied by a large number of investigators including Thorndike,[18] Pressey,[19] Skinner[20] and Bruner.[21] More recently Annett[22] has summarised research in the area. Fig 5 shows a very simplified diagram of some types of

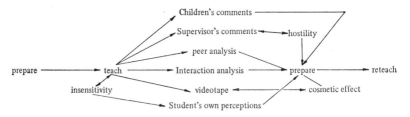

Fig 5   Six sources of feedback and resistive forces (insensitivity, hostility to supervisor and cosmetic effect)

feedback commonly used in micro-teaching. As examples there are three instances of possible resistive or preventive forces – the cosmetic effect, insensitivity and hostility to supervisor – which can prevent behaviour modification, but several other inhibiting factors could have been added. The types of feedback are worth considering separately.

Children's comments

Lewin[23] claimed that children as young as three or four could be even more sensitive than adults to certain situations within their experience, yet Domas and Tiedeman's survey of 672 studies of teacher effectiveness[24] showed that only seven investigators had

126

used pupils' ratings. In micro-teaching pupils' perception of the lesson, though not necessarily their ratings of its effectiveness, can provide very important information for the student about the impact of his teaching on the target group.

It has been the writer's own experience that pupils tend to provide less useful information through appraisals of effectiveness than in other ways. The Stanford Teacher Appraisal Guide attempts to enable children to make fine discriminations by accepting that they are inclined to rate generously and thus asking for judgements to be made on a 7 point scale with a bias towards the 'good' end. Point 3 is average and 4, 5, 6 and 7 are all above average. The full scale is (1) weak, (2) below average, (3) average, (4) strong, (5) superior, (6) outstanding and (7) truly exceptional.

Although ratings of effectiveness can be very useful for research purposes – for example, as indices of superior or inferior performance in the teach and reteach lessons – it is probably better for feedback purposes if children are offered a semi-structured form with two possibilities on it. First of all they can be invited to respond to specific statements tailored to suit the purpose of the particular skill being practised, consisting of items such as 'This teacher usually seemed pleased when we answered' (reinforcement), or 'This teacher asked questions that were a bit too hard for us to answer' (questions). Secondly they may be offered an opportunity to write anything they feel appropriate. One such possibility, phrased in a semi-projective way to encourage children to write more freely, is: 'Imagine that it is your job to help the teacher you have just had improve his teaching. Think about the lesson you have just had and write down what you would tell him about it. Remember you are trying to help him do it better next time.' This approach tends to produce its share of teacher stereotype statements about the need to be more strict, but if children are urged to think carefully about the particular lesson and teacher involved, they can produce surprisingly penetrating insights.

Supervisor's comments

Micro-teaching ranks among the most powerful supervision

tools yet devised. It offers power and control to be used or misused as the supervisor thinks fit, as well as limitless opportunities for self-indulgence to the megalomaniac with an exaggerated concept of himself as the paragon model. Not only is it possible to postulate the skills which the trainee should have, but the framework is such as to facilitate quantification of the extent to which he has acquired them in the reteach lessons. One can only state the potential horrors of misuse of the technique and urge that it should be used with sensitivity.

The initial temptation, given video playback facilities, is for the supervisor to run the whole tape and give a running commentary on it. This is to deny the validity of the students' perception and is certainly more directive than many would wish. This does not imply that the supervisor should adopt a totally non-directive role as this would leave many students floundering helplessly. The supervisor might consider the following objectives during the critique session:

1 Selecting from the videotape (having previously noted rev/ counter references during the lesson if possible) key events that will simplify the discussion. This includes the option not to use the videotape at all.
2 Helping the student evaluate the various sources of feedback available.
3 Helping the student clarify his own memories of the lesson.
4 Indicating, eliciting and discussing possible strategies for the subsequent lessons.

The dilemma inherent in the situation is not easily solved. Some students would welcome strong direction, while others would resist so strongly that the chances of behaviour change would be seriously reduced. Stones and Morris, commenting on a Johnson and Knaupp survey of student opinions on the role of the supervisor,[25] which showed that they expected expert guidance as well as opportunities to develop their own teaching persona, give a succinct and valuable analysis: 'Fair enough, but the freedom to do one's own thing is enlarged by the supervisor's early planning taking into account factors that the students are unlikely to apprehend. Essentially, of course, the main aim of the supervisor's work is precisely that: to cut the umbilical link as soon as possible without cutting off the students' pedagogical nourishment prematurely.'[26]

One other supervision tactic, as yet largely unexplored in the micro-teaching framework, would be that described by Caspari and Eggleston[27] and mentioned in Chapter 2, whereby the supervisor is not present for the lesson (and in this case perhaps for the video playback) but is more a consultant. The student has to describe the lesson, and the supervisor has to probe deeply to raise relevant issues.

Peer analysis

Little need be said about this kind of feedback, as the advantages of pairs and small groups of students working as teams have been discussed above, and joint critique sessions are the natural outcome. So much depends on the harmony or disunity within the group and also on the breadth and depth of the insights they are able to generate. Although peer analysis can replace supervisor analysis when available supervisory time is at a minimum, it will be seen as second best by those students who feel that novices will tend to pool their ignorance and lack the 'expert' analytical skills of the experienced supervisor. Several combinations are possible. Three students and a supervisor sharing critique sessions can work well, as can three students on their own. There is probably no optimum group size for these purposes, but groups of more than four students in a critique session might prove too formidable for the more timid students. Since supervisors at Stanford, usually experienced teachers working for higher degrees, received 30 hours of training before their first critique session, it does seem that teams of students working alone would need some preparation and advice about conducting analysis sessions before they began. Belt and Baird[28] report favourably on the degree of sensitisation which developed in groups where peers acted as supervisors and assessors.

Interaction analysis

Again little need be said except that, as a relatively objective source of information, interaction analysis data will often be valued by the students. Several relevant issues were raised in Chapter 3, but it can be restated here that when students are working together, one member of the team can act as coder and collect data during the live lesson. Alternatively a student can code his own videotape if he wishes.

Videotape

A more thorough appraisal of television facilities will be given in Chapter 7, but a number of issues are of immediate relevance. Britton and Leith[29] are among several writers who discuss the use of a director to select shots during filming.

Several methods of presentation are possible. A single fixed camera, favourably placed to cover both the teacher and class, is limited in what it offers but needs least attention during filming. Much more sensitive are methods which highlight particular aspects of interaction, but there are also concomitant difficulties with such techniques. If two or more cameras are used, one can be tracked on the teacher and another on the class, but then selections have to be made and it is possible to produce a very distorted record of a lesson. For example, the writer once used a student cameraman who tended to focus on what some writers have called 'task-irrelevant behaviour', that is children yawning, swinging their legs, scratching themselves or staring around the room. It was certainly useful to have a record of this, but it did suggest that the class was rather more inattentive than it was.

If split-screen facilities exist, several options are possible. Half the screen can show the teacher and the other half the class, and the student can thus watch either or both during the replay. Other possibilities are for the teacher to be 'framed' in the top right-hand quarter of the screen and the rest to show the whole class, or for the teacher and class to form the main part of the picture and the top corner to highlight particular children as crude thermometers of class response.

When split-screen possibilities are not available, the director has to choose which camera shot is shown, and it is therefore particularly useful if the supervisor can play this role, using his skill and insight to select what he judges to be the aspects of the lesson most worth recording.

Teams of students can share this facility, too, and again it provides a useful learning experience, as considerable thought must precede choice of camera shot, use of close-up, which element to focus on etc. A team of four students working together might involve one taking the lesson, one collecting interaction analysis data, one operating a camera and the fourth in the control room selecting what is preserved on videotape.

Trott[30] investigated the use of split-screen techniques at Berkshire College of Education and concluded that the most effective split was to have the bottom horizontal third of the picture showing the class and the top portion showing the student. He also reported that students wanted to see the whole (5 minute) videotape rather than selected extracts.

Student's own perceptions

Ultimately it is the student's own view of the original lesson and his interpretation of the other sources of feedback which will determine how he reteaches. Certainly the long-term effects will be contingent on his own perceptions, even though determined efforts by supervisors might induce short-term behaviour modifications. Consequently he should be given every facility to sharpen his powers of discrimination, to evaluate information, read cues, select from the mass of signals (often self-contradictory) and to control his own behaviour. The other modes of feedback described above all confirm or negate his own impressions, and in many cases highlight aspects of the lesson, such as the children's behaviour and attitudes, which eluded him at the time. All this is relevant to the section below.

RETEACH LESSON

There is so much to digest, given the volume of incidents which occur even in a brief 5 or 10 minute lesson, that a student may well need a minimum of an hour before he is ready to try out his ideas with a new group of children. On the other hand too long a delay would mean that he had forgotten some of the central issues emerging from his teach lesson.

The only points one would wish to stress about the reteach lesson are that it should take place under as nearly identical conditions to the first lesson as possible, that is with similar children in the same sized group and in the same environment; that it should be scrutinised in the same way as previously, with the same sources of feedback, ie children's reports, interaction analysis data, or whatever was used the first time; and that there should be a de-briefing session at which the supervisor, peer group and student concerned should attempt to evaluate the reteach lesson to see what changes emerge and to summarise what has been learned. Unless these procedures are adopted, the reteach becomes a formality, and a great deal of the potential value of micro-teaching can be lost. It is important that the student should feel he is learning something, even if his lessons appear not to be going as well as he had hoped, and it is in this area that the supervisor can perform a useful job of encouragement.

MINICOURSES

Attempts to develop materials using videotape technology developed at the Far West Laboratory for Educational Research and Development have been described by Borg,[31] Hutchins[32] and Ward,[33] among others. These self-contained training packages, called minicourses by their developers, comprise self-instructional materials primarily designed for experienced teachers to develop specific, precisely defined teaching skills which have been grouped, under the influence of the Stanford models, into what the authors call 'competency clusters'. Initial clusters are (1) *Questioning/ discussion*, including 'effective questioning in classroom discussion' (elementary and secondary levels), 'higher cognitive questioning' and 'divergent thinking'; (2) *Responding*, which has minicourses on 'role-playing in the upper elementary grades'; (3) *Management of independent, individualised learning*, which includes 'organising independent learning' at both primary and intermediate levels; (4) *Teaching reading*, with courses on 'teaching reading as decoding' and 'teaching reading as comprehension'; (5) *Teaching social studies*, which concerns itself with methods of enquiry by pupils into social and historical events and includes the mini-courses on 'higher cognitive questioning' and 'divergent thinking' mentioned above. Further units on 'presenting/explaining', 'developing children's oral language' and 'individualising instruction in mathematics' are already developed or nearing completion.

Each minicourse is based on the micro-teaching model of the skill under consideration being first studied, next observed, then practised and lastly refined. Typically the student will begin by reading the teacher's handbook about, for example, questions in the classroom. He will then watch a videotape or film in which the skill of questioning is described and illustrated, followed by a second videotape or film showing a teacher using the particular type of questions being studied. The student has to recognise and identify each skill as it occurs. Next he will prepare and teach a group of children (from one child to eight) for 10 minutes, filming his own lesson on videotape or recording it on sound tape. With the help of the special self-evaluation forms provided he plays back the lesson and analyses his own use of questions. Finally he reteaches another group, films the process and again evaluates his questioning skill. The whole micro-teaching cycle will have taken around 75 minutes a day for 7–9 days, to which must be added any videotape viewing and reading time he has spent.

The authors suggest that a coordinator should be responsible for organising each minicourse and acting as a consultant if the teacher required it. A plan is proposed whereby a local authority would allow 600 teachers to take a single minicourse in a 2-year period.[34] When, in a field test of the first minicourse, ninety-six Florida teachers were asked to compare the minicourse with other kinds of in-service training they had received, 76 per cent rated it as 'much better' than other in-service training, 22 per cent as 'better' and the remaining 2 per cent as 'on a par'.[35] A group of seventy teachers at Livingston University were asked to rate their minicourse programme on a 6-point scale, and sixty-four rated it 'very worthwhile' or 'outstanding', while only three rated it 'poor' or 'very poor'.[36]

It is not unusual, of course, to achieve high ratings of approval on the early stages of development of package materials, even self-instructional ones, where the enthusiasm and energy of the designers can readily infect those undergoing the experiences, but even if such minicourses are not judged to be appropriate outside the United States, the possibilities of a largely self-instructional and flexible package are clear for all to see. There is nothing to prevent anyone in teacher training from developing his own materials for the group of students receiving training, whether they be experienced or inexperienced. These materials could be cheap or expensive, depending on the facilities available, and, given a wide variety of other personal contacts with supervisors and tutors, could provide interesting exploration material for students, provided their options were kept open rather than narrowed by the programmed instruction format.

SOME RESEARCH FINDINGS

There are too many research findings to summarise here and they are of dubious value. For example, it would be of small concern to know that a group of students, after being filmed and badgered by their tutor during a session on reinforcement, did in fact make greater use of reinforcement on the reteach lesson. Some of the enquiries do have relevance, like Ward's study of 141 secondary training institutions in the United States,[37] which found that increases in the student's self-confidence, enthusiasm and under-standing of the teaching process were most frequently reported.

Studies of the supervisor by Koran[38] and Stewig[39] have tended to concentrate on the supervisor's role as the initiator of behaviour change. Until more long-term studies are available, however, any short-term evidence is of limited value. It is interesting to note that the Far West Laboratory evaluation of the minicourses does include follow-up studies after 6 months to help provide evidence about longer-term behaviour changes.

Olivero[40] found that students who saw videotapes of their lessons and discussed them with supervisors showed greater behaviour changes on the reteach lesson than those having dis-cussions with supervisors but not seeing video playbacks.

The writer[41] investigated the effects of video playback and interaction analysis separately and in combination. It was found that video playback and interaction analysis feedback produced greater improvements in children's ratings as well as greatest behaviour change.

Certainly more research is needed into the effects of supervisors, and of feedback from other sources, but equally important is the role of the student's personality in modification of behaviour. In addition the long-term effects of these influences are of great concern.

ENDNOTE

The scaled-down format of micro-teaching offers real possibilities for those concerned with teacher training to help their students modify their teaching and try to make it, to their joint best judgement, more effective. It is open to abuse, as it offers the supervisor opportunities for real power and control if he chooses to exploit them. It also can make him partially obsolete if he is not to be one of the sources of feedback or if the materials designed are self-instructional.

At its best it can give the student a gentle but meaningful introduction to real teaching, or allow him to focus on known weaknesses if he has already taught. At its worst it will segment a set of skills, which the Gestalt psychologist would see more as a totality, in such a way as to prevent him effectively reassembling them and himself as a teacher.

Perhaps this is the main source of uneasiness in those who reject it as a usable technique. It does seem to suggest that skills can be identified by someone else in a general way and grafted on to the recruit one by one. The student's own reading of his needs, such as his anxiety about 'discipline', would be seen to be too diffuse, to have crudely subsumed other more precise elements such as the use of reinforcement, variety of stimulus, interaction style, questioning etc. Yet maybe, instinctively, this is where one should begin, with the more loosely defined higher-inference variables such as warmth, discipline and enthusiasm. It would

135

be a pity if a promising technique such as micro-teaching were to ossify around the Stanford skills at an early stage. One hopes there will be creative, energetic and ingenious explorations of all the possibilities in the future.

For notes to this chapter see pp 208–10.

5 Simulation and Role-playing

For a variety of reasons simulation techniques have been used in all kinds of teaching contexts for hundreds of years. The main advantages claimed are, firstly, that it enables the learner to practise a skill, or learn a principle, in conditions of safety. This is particularly important where potential danger to life or health is involved, hence the use of flight simulators in pilot training and artificial heads and teeth on which trainee dentists can practise filling and drilling. Secondly, he can be closely supervised, so that learning can be more effective than if he were in the real situation away from supervision. This is particularly helpful where supervision in the real-life situation is impossible or extremely difficult; where the presence of a supervisor would lead to substantial changes in the 'naturalness' of events, which can happen in classrooms; or where the supervisor is not easily able to stop proceedings in order to analyse errors or to enable the trainee to make further attempts, which is an option not normally available during conventional school practice. The third advantage, therefore, which has just been mentioned, is the facility to try again if one's first efforts are unsuccessful.

There are other regular benefits, and some which are occasional and incidental, though equally welcome. For example, simulation facilities are often provided in the training institution, which means that students and supervisors do not have to travel extensively. It also ensures that the group of trainees can share experiences, and that the theoretical parts of the course can more readily be related to the practical. A degree of control is possible in that the supervisor can establish conditions which compel the trainee to use a certain skill, consider an important issue, or learn to consult others in the group, whereas in real situations it might be possible for him to avoid confronting the more painful matters of concern until the day when he can no longer avoid conflict. By then it would be too late for him to regret his lack of experience in dealing with similar cases.

Finally, and of particular importance where establishment of high group morale is important, despite the conflicts which can sometimes emerge, there is a real possibility that strong group excitement and enthusiasm will develop as trainees not only pick up the skills needed but often produce ideas of real quality, gratifying to themselves and their supervisors.

Common applications of the technique include wargames, for amateurs or professionals, where it is possible for Napoleon to win the Battle of Waterloo, and indeed *Kriegsspiele* were used by the Prussians as early as the eighteenth century and more regularly in the nineteenth. Businessmen increasingly use simulations to train new recruits and to introduce experienced entrepreneurs to new methods. For example, advertising executives might design a campaign for a fictitious new brand of perfume, salesmen might devise new marketing methods for an imaginary product, or managing directors might reorganise an invented ailing business concern to make it more profitable.

In the training of teachers simulations are well worth using for many of the above reasons, but there is a further argument in favour of the techniques. Increasingly children themselves are being invited to learn via simulations and games. Taylor and Walford,[1] in a comprehensive survey of materials and procedures developed for school use, describe a wide variety of commercially produced packaged materials enabling groups of children to consider matters such as conservation, farming, newspaper editing, developing countries, the economy, international relations and many others.

There will be an analysis in this chapter of some of the materials and ideas already available for teacher training, but the main emphasis will be on do-it-yourself ideas. Although commercially produced packaged materials are certainly useful, in that they are usually professionally finished and have been field-tested, there are a number of disadvantages. Usually they have been designed

138

with a particular group of students in mind, in which case they will need adapting for other groups. If the design of a package presupposes that the users are American junior high school teachers, it may have little to offer British or Australian secondary school trainees. On the other hand it may only need minor modifications to be appropriate. The main advantages of materials home-made in the college or training institution are the same as for domestically produced televised or filmed materials, namely that (1) the degree of commitment by the authors is high and therefore their enthusiasm is likely to make the exercise work, and (2) that the materials can be more sensitively tailored to the needs of the trainees concerned.

SIMULATION IN TEACHER TRAINING

A distinction needs to be made between role-playing exercises, where, by playing the parts of a teacher or members of the class, the students re-create the atmosphere of a real classroom and hence are concerned primarily with exploring classroom dynamics, and activities whose issues are to do with school life, such as pastoral care, organisation or curriculum planning, which clearly concern children's learning and well-being but do not actually involve students in playing the part of the learner. Role-playing exercises are much closer to the role-playing drama classes now used extensively in psychotherapy, and based on the writings of influential thinkers and practitioners such as Moreno[2] and Klein.[3] Here the role-player learns to feel empathy for others and hence, it is hoped, develops better relations in his day-to-day life. The expectation from psycho-drama with student teachers is that by reliving some of the frustrations, excitement and occasional bewilderment of being a pupil they will be better sensitised to children's needs.

Tansey[4] and Unwin[5] have written about some of the applications of simulation techniques in the training of teachers, and Stones and Morris[6] refer to them more briefly. One of the best known and most widely reported simulations was developed by Kersch,[7] who had previously had considerable experience of simulation procedures in the armed forces. The Kersch simulation is expensive and complex, requiring several projectors, a rear projection screen and a great deal of supervisor time. The students are assumed to be under the care of Mr Land, a teacher of a sixth grade. They have access to the complete school records of every one of the twelve-year-old children in this class, and they are then put in certain problem situations facing the rear projection screen as if they were the teacher at the front of the class. A scene unfolds and the trainee has to make responses. The supervisor controls the multiple projectors and selects the next film sequence in accordance with the student's behaviour.

One would need to have seen this in action to be able to make a sound evaluation, but it does appear that the Kersch simulator, while interesting, can only have limited sensitivity as a training instrument, since the filmed materials predetermine some of the options. For example, Kersch's first problem involves a child approaching the teacher to ask if he can stay in school during playtime because he was ill the previous week. The records show that the child is of low ability, sensitive to criticism and requires a lot of attention. Although in reality the responses by the teacher and subsequently the child would be contingent on a vast complex of minute and barely detectable signals contained in tone of voice, facial expressions, movement, gesture and verbal content of message, the only broad possibilities allowed for are (a) the teacher defers to authority, accepts the note warmly and says he will consult Mr Land the regular teacher, (b) he rejects the approach and refers the child directly to Mr Land, (c) he asks for the note and agrees, anticipating that Mr Land would approve, and (d) he accepts the note but is abrupt in his manner. The child's responses are limited to nodding and returning to his seat or reaching into his pocket and delivering the note. Clearly it would take vast numbers of filmed responses and loaded projectors even to begin to approximate the real event. By the third or fourth event in sequence millions of combinations of interdependent transactions would need to have been provided. Refinement of the options down to even as few as six may inevitably lead to over-simplificaion, stereotyping and straitjacketing, though this judgement, it should be repeated, is based on written descriptions of the procedures and not on the writer's live experience of it. Perhaps if the behaviour of groups of children were as predictable as the behaviour of aircraft in response to manipulation of the controls, the Kersch simulator might be very real. At its best it might well enable students to examine problems and the possible outcomes of certain acts of behaviour by the teacher despite its limited capabilities.

A discussion approach to classroom problems is possible through the programme devised by Cruickshank[8] at the University of Tennessee. After seeing filmed material showing the fictitious Longacre Elementary School, Madison, students take turns to play Pat Taylor, the ambiguity of whose name enables the role to be assumed by either male or female students. The problems range over a wide area, including matters to do with pastoral care, curriculum planning and teaching methods.

Rather than produce a catalogue of kits and packages, however, I would prefer to indicate broad outlines of possible applications of simulation procedures, so that those concerned with the education and training of teachers may, if they wish, design their own ideas around them.

CLASSROOM SIMULATION BASED ON ROLE-PLAYING

One of the most useful methods, and the nearest approach to socio- or psycho-drama, is to simulate a real classroom with the group of trainees acting the parts both of learners and teachers. Many variations are possible, and, provided the group is willing to suspend its communal disbelief and accept the inevitable unreality, much of value can emerge. Consider, for example, the following three examples, based on my own experiences with groups of languages specialists.

Example 1 A group of trainee language teachers is being taught Russian by George, one of their members who knows the language well. None of the others knows any Russian. George tries to teach a word which is difficult to pronounce and asks Felicity, a quiet but tenacious student, to say it. She has two attempts which

George rejects. 'No, say it again, Felicity, and this time listen carefully.' Felicity's attempts begin to get worse as she fails to pick out which element of the word she is mispronouncing. As the law of diminishing returns begins to apply, Felicity sniggers at her seventh or eighth attempt and this angers George. 'Come on, Felicity, and this time stop fooling about.' Felicity protests she really cannot do any better and has a final attempt which George accepts grudgingly, but he seems unaware that Felicity is genuinely near to tears. Later Felicity is teaching German and George is a pupil. She deliberately asks him a difficult word and makes him pronounce it several times, reprimanding him each time. The strained attentiveness of the other members in the group suggests that they recognise vengeance when they see it, and I share the feelings of discomfort.

Example 2 John tells the group they are to pretend they are having their first ever German lesson. He employs a widely used audio-visual course unit one filmstrip and tape and the role-playing German graduates sail through it at impressive speed, planting occasional deliberate mistakes. In the discussion which ensues most are convinced that they played the role of beginners well and that most classes of at least average ability could be expected to make similar progress in their first ever lesson. At this stage Ruth, who has lived in Yugoslavia for 2 years, produces a tape she has made containing the identical vocabulary and express-ions but in Serbo-Croat. The filmstrip is shown again with the new sound tape. Chaos ensues, cries of 'Play that phrase again' or 'I didn't catch the last bit' prevent Ruth from getting more than half-way through a very bedraggled set of class responses. In subsequent discussion occasional arguments that Serbo-Croat is a harder language than German or that the second tape was of poorer quality begin to sound a little thin.

Example 3 The last simulation session of the term just before Christmas sees the 'class' in a festive mood. Jerry, one of the more confident members of the group, is coping well until Mark and Ian fool around once too often and begin to irritate him. He turns to write on the blackboard, and, hearing laughter, he whirls round angrily. 'Marianne, get out of the room and I'll see you at the end

142

of the lesson.' Marianne is the quietest, best behaved member of the class who has barely said a word all term.

Each of these examples occurred with the 'pupils' in unassigned roles – in other words they could choose to misbehave or to be cooperative. The examples show similar and yet different aspects of classroom-type role-plays. The first incident was, at first, simply going to provide discussion matter along the lines, 'Is it worth pressing a child to pronounce a word as many as eight or ten times when he is clearly not getting any better?' But then real personal hostility developed, with the emergence of additional and heavier issues about authority, victimisation and insensitivity which were uncomfortable to handle. Since teachers do sometimes indulge in persecution of individuals who fail to please, perhaps it is as well to raise the issue at the training stage via a real shared example, but as tutor I found it a very difficult one to handle and I spent a long time pondering whether to continue role-playing with the particular group. As it happened, the group concerned was very cohesive and even the two protagonists learned to tolerate each other.

The second example shows simulation working both badly and well. On the first run-through the group was doing rather too well, and it would have been part of the tutor's function to point out, had the matter not been raised, that most real classes of beginners would have had greater difficulties and that, although they had tried to make 'errors', these would normally have been more frequent and of different kinds. Knowing that this can happen, however, I had asked Ruth to prepare the Serbo-Croat tape. Suddenly, for real learners, the amount of explanation, repetition, use of the tape recorder, teacher's amplification and clarification, all became critical because as real learners the students could not function unless conditions were favourable.

The third example was both unexpected and interesting. Mouths fell open when Marianne was dispatched from the room, with surprise that Jerry needed to send someone out at all and because of his choice of victim. A great deal of discussion about 'discipline' ensued.

It is, of course, difficult for students to play groups of children with exactitude. Yet what constantly astonishes one is the convincing reality of what occurs after the first session or two. Roles are naturally assumed and sustained week after week and many of the issues growing out of the 'teaching' are as real as if they had occurred with a class of children. So long as the sessions are prepared carefully, analysed and followed up, much valuable experience can be shared.

My own pattern has been to let students know a week in advance that they are teaching the following week. Together tutor and student discuss subject matter and strategies, relating these where possible to what is being dealt with in other sessions during the week. The 'teacher' begins his 15–20 minute session by telling the group what kind of class they are, eg a group of thirteen-year-old beginners in German, 'O' level class in history, mixed ability nine-year-olds doing project. After that the 'children' are free to assume any natural role within the given framework, and the lesson proceeds. At its worst it can be strained and halting, at its best astonishingly real.

Assigning roles is a legitimate possibility, and this can be done where the tutor is hoping to raise certain issues or highlight points of interest. Adelman and Walker[9] have developed games with assigned roles for the participants based on a rationale influenced by Keith Johnson's half-mask classes at the Royal Court Theatre in 1962–3, Ed Berman's 'Interaction' initiation techniques, and the writings of Argyle,[10] Smith and Geoffrey,[11] Cage[12] and Rogers.[13] As described above, the teacher prepares his lesson, but 'pupils' each receive a card containing an instruction such as, 'Try to change the content and/or direction of the lesson', 'Every third question the teacher asks, put your hand up', 'Every class has ringleaders who are the centre of attention. Try to identify the ringleaders and urge them on', 'Try to become the centre of attraction in the class, but always do as the teacher asks you'. In addition, several can be instructed to do as the teacher asks or play a 'free' role according to inclination. In another game non-verbal aspects of communication are cued. 'Pupils' are instructed to lean back in their chairs, rub their chins, yawn, twiddle their thumbs or look around the room. More attentive non-verbal behaviour can also be cued.

Amidon[14] has developed similar communication games related to particular interaction analysis systems. Such games would include conditioning the teacher to explore a type of behaviour by instructions such as, 'Before making a contribution, you must first clarify what the previous speaker has said'. A known garrulous participant can be told he must take a 15 or 20 minute lesson but not speak more than 50 per cent of the time. Stopwatch control ensures that he is 'gonged' if he should use his time allocation, and he has to endure the rest in silence.

Role assignment and conditioned games need particularly sensitive handling if they are not to produce totally unreal situations or become nothing more than anodyne time-fillers, and it is frequently more spontaneous to use unassigned roles; but since individual needs will tend to vary, those wishing to use role-playing will have to explore all methods available for themselves.

Some cautionary warnings are also necessary. Setting up and running role-playing sessions is very demanding, and the leader needs to believe quite strongly that it is worthwhile. Anyone using it without conviction is likely to find his own lack of enthusiasm rapidly communicated to the group. The situation can put quite a severe burden on the more apprehensive student, for whom it is little consolation to know that he might benefit from the experience if only he will try it. After 7 years of experience with role-playing, which I began partly because of a relative lack of facilities for students to gain specialist teaching experience before teaching practice, I have found that it ran well enough on five occasions, one year it was possible but not too successful and on the seventh occasion with a group of particularly shy and tense students it was strained and unprofitable and I had not the slightest hesitation in terminating it after only a few sessions. On the other hand it should be pointed out that some of the best discussions about teaching I have been able to participate in have arisen naturally from these shared role-plays.

Finally, if children are not available for micro-teaching as described in the previous chapter, then peer-group instruction can sometimes be an acceptable substitute.

OTHER FORMS OF CLASSROOM SIMULATION

If students are not to role-play classroom scenes themselves, it is still possible to raise relevant issues to do with teacher-pupil relations and classroom dynamics by other means. It is worth describing in some detail one of the videotapes I made for this purpose.

The Lovegrove incident

The question of discipline has been shown on numerous occasions to be of great, even obsessive, concern to students before their teaching practice. It is easy to argue, when students ask about discipline, that if lessons are interesting, disciplinary problems do not arise, or that one has dealt with discipline already at length, though not as a separate topic, under headings such as 'lesson preparation', 'teacher-pupil interaction', 'objectives' or 'home background'. Yet to the student teacher discipline *is* a separate identifiable topic as well as a source of anxiety. It concerns questions such as, 'Why do lessons go wrong?', 'Why do some children fool about and not pay attention?' and 'What do you do if things do go wrong?' The reply that such questions are unanswerable in general terms is a lame one.

We had tried discussing the question of discipline, giving tips, case studies and analysis of students' own experiences. We decided to make a film of a lesson going badly and use it as an introduction to a lengthy session on the topic of class control. A class of boys in a local school was used and a 20 minute videotape was made with a portable television camera around the following story line.

Mr Fox, a probationer teacher of English, is taking 2A first lesson after lunch. They are to study a comprehension passage and later write something of their own on a similar theme. After a few minutes Lovegrove and three of his friends burst in late. They have been at the tuck shop and are insolent as they take up their seats

146

in the back corner. As the lesson progresses, unruliness gets worse. It begins with note-passing and sniggering, later there is pellet-throwing, with Lovegrove playing a very active part. He offers to answer questions, but is often ignored. When he does answer, he often gives flippant replies or makes a joke. Finally Mr Fox discovers he has not done his homework and gives him the standard school punishment, a debit mark in his record book. As Mr Fox returns to the front of the class, a pellet hits him. He turns swiftly, seizes a book and hits Lovegrove on the head with it. The lesson ends with the class in sullen silence.

The film was made as an improvisation in four separate 5 minute segments. Apart from Lovegrove and his unruly friends, some of the other members of the class were assigned particular roles. Six or eight were instructed to be supportive of the teacher, to 'shush' the wayward members once in a while, and to try to give good answers to the teacher's questions. Three or four were instructed to aid the Lovegrove quartet, and the rest were to follow their inclination in as natural a way as possible. In addition they were told not to overplay their naughtiness in the early stages of the lesson. The result was a frighteningly real looking lesson with superlative acting by a class who, like many other lively groups of thirteen-year-old boys, had done their fair share of lesson sabotage.

The film has been used in several ways. On two occasions it was followed by live role-plays, when tutors in the department enacted the roles of Mr Fox the probationer teacher, the headmaster, the head of the English department and Lovegrove's counsellor. This role-play began with the head explaining to the head of English that Lovegrove's father had written to complain about an incident in class. Mr Fox was interviewed by the head and head of department together, and finally the counsellor was summoned to give Lovegrove's account of the incident. After this 20 minute live role-play students went into groups to discuss the film and the issues raised. In a plenary session the central characters answered questions both in and out of role. In the course of such discussions points raised by students concerned the subject matter of the lesson, Lovegrove's background, group dynamics, authority, the roles of the head and head of department, and many other important aspects of classroom relations.

Another option with this kind of film is for the role-playing to be done not by tutors and then discussed but by groups of four students. This would demand extra documentation, so that each student has copies of the letter from Lovegrove's father, a report to the head written by the head of English on Mr Fox's probationary year, Lovegrove's report and school record, and samples of his recent written work in English.

Our main fear when we first viewed the film was that it might horrify some of the more timid students, and possibly put them off teaching, confirming in their minds that the job was too hazardous. Although there is always tension in the discussions which follow the film, many students report relief that they have been able to use the experience shown to talk about their own anxieties. In any case, as the disorder is, on the whole, relatively mild, showing only the chaos that occurs in any lessons where a lively class suffering from boredom engineers its own entertainments, it is not too different from what many students have participated in themselves. As a means of provoking discussion on the issue of discipline the technique of film followed by role-play is very effective.

Critical incidents

Corsini and Howard[15] have written on the critical incidents technique developed by Flanagan[16] and later used in research into teachers' characteristics by Ryans.[17] For research purposes the investigator would ask large numbers of children, teachers, administrators and students to recall critical incidents from lessons which either showed effective results leading to a successful conclusion as judged by the person reporting or led to failure. The investigator would analyse the incidents, try to extract salient features, and finally classify acts judged to produce a successful or unsuccessful outcome.

A modification of this technique enables it to be used by student teachers. Again it involves videotape and partial role-playing. A videotape like the Lovegrove incident can be made specially, or any appropriate piece of film, or even live student role-playing, can be the starting point. The task of the group of students is to identify critical incidents which seems illustrative of effectiveness or ineffectiveness by the teacher, but they have to assume a particular role to do this. Using the Lovegrove incident film, for example, such assigned roles might include Lovegrove himself, Mr Fox the teacher, a well behaved member of the class who resents people spoiling lessons, Lovegrove's best friend, a local authority adviser who believes that teachers who cannot keep order should not pass their probationary year, a head of English who is trying to help the teacher with a class which he himself has found difficult, and Lovegrove's father. Each has to highlight critical incidents as if he were the person concerned, and either write a report or take part in discussion. Analysis can be both in and out of role, that is Lovegrove's 'father' might observe that he was not going to permit anyone to hit his son and the student teacher playing the role might later agree with, qualify or contradict this if his own feelings differ. It is often best to begin analysis in role and then finish off the discussion out of role.

There are infinite possibilities for improvisation, and topics of concern to students can be chosen. Videotapes might be made around subjects such as the two examples given below.

Example 1 In Westgate Primary School Mrs Shaw is trying to obtain greater flexibility by using the corridor outside her classroom and the cloakroom for children to work. Difficulties encountered and shown on videotape include children not working when out in the cloakroom, caretaker grumbling about mess in the corridor, parent reporting seeing children outside the school gate and Mrs James in adjacent classroom not agreeing with methods used. Allocated roles in discussion might be Mrs Shaw, Mrs James, a child who likes the flexibility, a child who dislikes it, and a supportive head, HMI or LEA adviser who is willing to help with ideas to improve soundproofing, provide suitable furnishings, curtains, display space, resources area etc.

Example 2 Exchester Comprehensive School has gone over to mixed ability groups in the first year. Videotape shows that Mr Jackson is teaching chemistry in a largely traditional manner, but

149

he finds that several children cannot write very well and that the brighter children get bored. Assigned discussion roles could include Mr Jackson, a head who is for mixed ability groups but is not a chemist, a head of chemistry who is against mixed ability groups, a neutral HMI who knows a great deal about mixed ability group teaching (this role might have to be played by the tutor, but a student might read up some information beforehand), a child who is bewildered by much of what goes on, and a bright child who enjoys chemistry but occasionally finds the lessons too slow-moving.

Student teachers in the course of the discussion can make penetrating observations often with a refreshing insight unfettered by years of resigned acceptance of current practices. Frequently such revelations give a natural lead into the extensive psychology and sociology of education literature, prompting one to discover more about the phenomena which have been observed. For example, the 'ripple effects', that is the effects that certain control techniques exercised by the teacher on one misbehaving child can have on the others watching, phenomena investigated and reported by Kounin and Gump,[18] may often be detected by 'Lovegrove's friend' or 'a well behaved member of the class'.

NON-CLASSROOM SIMULATIONS

The activities described above were all based on classroom interactions and incidents, but there is wide scope, using simulation techniques, for consideration of issues to do with school life which do not require a videotape of a lesson, staged or otherwise, and do not require participants to role-play teachers and children giving and receiving instruction. Some of the problems are of greater concern to experienced teachers than novices, but may be used or modified for use with both groups.

In-basket techniques

Exercises based on what a business executive might find in his in-tray one Monday morning were developed originally for head-masters and administrators in education to enable them to analyse and compare their decision-making processes. A typical problem might consist of two memos to the head – one from the school caretaker saying that he is fed up with Mr Brown the art master leaving the art room in a mess, often being there after school hours and even being rude to himself and the cleaning staff when they try to get on with their job; the second from Mr Brown asking whether the school exists for children to learn or not, and objecting to the rude way in which the caretaker asks him to leave whenever he is finishing off work with keen pupils after 4 o'clock. Although local solutions would obviously depend on the personalities of Mr Brown and the caretaker and the effectiveness of the head, the in-basket has proved to be a stimulating technique for enabling established and aspiring heads to share ideas and look more objectively at their own administrative and personnel management skills.

Such personnel problems may be a little remote from the interests of new or even experienced teachers unless they are concerned with administration and man management. Curricular matters, pastoral care and relations with colleagues are more fruitful areas to explore with these groups.

Curriculum

Curriculum planning in schools demands a number of high-level skills. These include the pre-operational skills of inventiveness cooperation with colleagues and planning, followed by the execution of ideas in the classroom and subsequent evaluation. Many of these skills can be practised under simulation conditions. Some examples have been cited above, but further examples are given below.

Example 1 This first example is taken from the excellent Science Teacher Education Project[19] and shows how the in-basket technique can be used to initiate a discussion about aims in science teaching. Students have copies of two letters sent to the head of a comprehensive school. The first letter is signed by two members of the science department and reads as follows:

Head
We do not like to go over our Head of Department but we do feel that it is time we discussed one of our problems with you.

151

Ever since his arrival at the beginning of the year, Ken Wheeler has been trying to be the new broom. Over and over he has implied (or actually stated) that our teaching of science is old-fashioned, and that we are doing harm to our pupils because we are 'hindering their conceptual development'. He is insisting that we abandon the methods we have built up and perfected over many years' teaching, and expects us, at the drop of a hat, to try out his pet theory. What is more he fails to praise our work to the impressionable beginners in the department.

We have seen too many bandwagons come and go to be impressed by this latest one. Our textbooks and methods have enabled us to prepare many a boy and girl for passing their examinations, and we would not want to see our academic standards, and therefore our pupils, suffer.

No doubt when Mr Wheeler has had our experience, he will be the wiser for it. But meanwhile, we fear that his insistence on the new approach will set back the standards of the Department for many years.

Could you please persuade Mr Wheeler to think again?

R. Whitehead
C. Able

The second letter is from Ken Wheeler expressing his point of view:

Dear Head

I am sorry to have to bring this problem to your attention, but for a whole term now I have been struggling against reactionary opposition within my department, and my frustration has come to the point where I must seek your support.

As you know, I am very keen that we should introduce the Nuffield approach into the school, beginning with the junior forms initially, and then extending up the school; combining this with the judicial introduction of certain topics into Upper School work as soon as possible. In this I have the full support of Brenda Crowhurst and I know that I have yours also.

However, others of my staff are refusing to have anything to do with this, and are insisting on remaining with the traditional texts in chemistry and in physics. I have held a number of meetings with the department where we were to have discussed the scheme I proposed, and where we could explore the difficulties of teaching with the new materials and concepts. However, most of the time the 'opposition' just don't turn up. And when I ask them why not, they just say that they haven't time to 'waste' if they are going to prepare their pupils for the examinations.

It is absolutely vital that our Departmental Scheme of Work has unanimous support – it cannot work unless all the classes are involved eventually. And we don't want to lose Brenda to a more progressive school if we can help it; she is a first-rate teacher and greatly appreciated by the pupils.

I have done what I can, but I can't get anywhere with these obstructionists. Can you get these teachers to cooperate?

Ken Wheeler

In addition to the text of these two letters students are given the following background notes about the staff concerned:

KENNETH WHEELER: Age 32. MA, BSc (Oxon). First-class honours in biochemistry, Postgraduate Certificate in Education (Cantab). Has taught in various schools, and for one year lectured in science in a College of Education. Appointed Head of Science nearly a year ago, and now a teacher-tutor for the Area Training Organisation. Married, with three children.

DICK WHITEHEAD: Aged 44. Two-year trained (PE and Science), Teacher's Certificate. Taught in several secondary modern schools with 'good examination success' before appointment to his present position 6 years ago.

CHARLES ABLE: Age 58. BSc (General) London. Taught in grammar school for 23 years before being appointed to this school (before comprehensive reorganisation) in 1960. Applied for the position of head of department in 1965 and 1970, but was not short-listed on either occasion.

BRENDA CROWHURST: Age 24. BSc Hons Cl ii(i) (Leeds), Postgraduate Certificate in Education (Nottingham). In second year of first post.

Students are invited to read the letters and background information and then analyse differences in aims of the teachers, to list

153

issues raised and to imagine how, if they were the headmaster concerned, they would tackle the problem. The last of these assignments is perhaps of more peripheral concern to a trainee, but nevertheless this is an example of a well documented and legitimate use of simulation in the field of curriculum study.

Example 2 Working groups of four students from various subject backgrounds explore joint curriculum planning. Astley Hill Middle School has decided to try a one-term team-teaching experiment with the top year group (twelve- to thirteen-year-olds) around the theme 'Man and Machines'. Four teachers, specialists in history, science, English and geography, are to work with 100 children.

Students work in their groups of four to plan timetable requirements, rooms, content of course, modes of teaching, including actual assignment of responsibility for particular elements of the course, resources etc.

This is a substantial assignment which can easily absorb a whole day, but normally many issues of importance arise. The importance of long-term planning because of timetable constraints emerges early in the discussions, and suggestions involving hire of film, packaged materials, visiting speakers, home-made resources and visits further underline this aspect. Since the planning groups frequently opt for blocks of time on the timetable, much careful thought is needed for suitable teaching strategies to be produced.

Ideally the group would plan their term's programme with a particular group of children in mind and then go on to carry it out in the school concerned. They would thus be able to evaluate their planning in the light of their subsequent experiences, and, more importantly, be able to modify their original plan if necessary as the term progressed. This brings the exercise much nearer to reality, but the full facilities to carry planning to fruition may not always be available. Even without the payoff, however, the planning exercise is of value, and the presence of a supervising tutor or experienced teacher can serve both to tighten the thinking behind the schemes and hypothesise about likely outcomes and difficulties.

Example 3 An analysis of methods of teaching reading. In

response to a report suggesting that reading standards are declining Miss Wallace, headmistress of the Lily Douglas Infants' School, calls together her staff so that methods of teaching reading in the school can be reappraised. The local Primary Schools Adviser has visited the school several times and written to the head.

Students act as class teachers, with one playing the headmistress. The task is to discuss reading schemes, teaching methods and children's records. An extract from a report on reading standards would be needed. Such reports appear regularly and are not always critical, but this document can be taken from, for example, the survey by Start and Wells.[20] The letter from the Primary Schools Adviser might run as follows:

Dear Miss Wallace,
I am delighted that you and your staff are considering a critical reappraisal of methods of teaching reading in the school, and that you have given me the opportunity to help you in your planning. As you know I have spent half days with most of the teachers in the school and I would offer the following suggestions. First of all the staff might like to look through the four reading schemes we discussed. In their different ways each of the four might be a distinct improvement on what you use at present. Secondly you could watch and discuss the videotape on the teaching of reading made by the advisory staff in conjunction with the teachers' centre and the college of education. Thirdly, and this is of special importance, there is the question of recording children's progress. I noticed that most of the staff had no complete record of reading progress, except for Miss Hargreaves, who kept detailed accounts and also gave a termly reading test. I am sure there will be plenty here to keep you busy for a few weeks! If there is anything else I can do to help, please let me know. As ever I am glad to have the opportunity to work in a school such as yours where the teachers are so willing to take a regular look at issues of professional concern like this.

Yours sincerely,

Alice Norwood

Primary Adviser

Examples of the four reading schemes referred to above will be needed. Any current materials can be used, and the number available might be more or less than four.

A videotape, as mentioned in the letter, might show three different teachers hearing children read, including, for example, one who corrects every mistake immediately, one who ignores errors and only supplies words the child cannot provide, and one who encourages the child to sound the phonic components of words he cannot read. There are numerous possibilities for such a videotape, though the exercise can be undertaken without the tape. If available, however, it does enable discussion to centre on teaching tactics as well as other factors of importance.

Finally, examples of reading tests, including both diagnostic and progress types, will be required.

This simulation is perhaps best done as a series, because consideration of reading schemes, teaching methods and testing and recording progress raises too many important issues.

Example 4 A creative thinking exercise. In response to the introduction of a new examination in French which gives 50 per cent of the marks for oral competence, a group of teachers are to plan teaching strategies which are likely to produce greater oral competence from their children. Groups of five students specialising in French play the parts of French teachers in structured and unstructured productive thinking sessions. One person acts as secretary, noting down all ideas that are produced for subsequent evaluation.

Nothing is more exciting for the student teacher than to feel a genuine sense of innovation or originality, even if, in practice, ideas which to him are novel have been used elsewhere. If teaching is to hold lifelong interest for members of the profession, and, indeed, if the profession is to remain or become a dynamic one, interest in scrutinising, accepting and developing new techniques must be of prime importance. Doing more than merely learning to live with the discomforts of change may become the foremost survival requirement for new teachers. Consequently the confidence and the excitement of inventing and exploring new methods and techniques need to be experienced at an early stage.

Torrance,[21] Mooney[22] and Getzels and Jackson[23] are among many who have discussed whether creative skills can be actively fostered in educational settings, and Cropley,[24] describing some research into methods of stimulating ideational fluency, cites a number of studies where certain teaching tactics were shown to produce gains in a variety of creative skills.

Among the most popular techniques for enabling groups of adults to produce more and better ideas is the one known as 'brainstorming'. In an atmosphere of mutual support and with criticism of members' suggestions not permitted, participants produce as many ideas as possible in response to the set task or problem. All ideas are noted by a group secretary. Parnes and Meadow[25] found that not only did training in such activities increase participants' scores on tests of creative problem solving, but that for as long as four years after training had been completed the increased skill in problem solving persisted.[26]

Deferment of evaluation certainly facilitates spontaneous generation of new and often unusual ideas, but many students find the total absence of structure inhibiting. It is possible in such cases to keep the basic evaluation-free concept of brainstorming, and at the same time offer a degree of structure which has a mildly restrictive but not suffocating effect on the group.

Among many possible structures for a curriculum-planning exercise are the following three

Example 5   Think of the perfect situation. By speculating about perfection, even if this is unobtainable or over-costly, the group is proposing directions of change. For example, if in designing the perfect motor car a participant were to propose that it should travel at a million miles per hour and never be involved in an accident, this would reveal that he valued speed and safety. Even if his proposals exceed the likely bounds of present-day manufacturing competence, greater safety and speed might be obtainable.

With the problem of oral French, a student might propose that each child be given opportunities to converse with a French person. This could produce ideas such as the use of local French housewives, au pair girls, other expatriates, older children who speak

157

good French, a school exchange, with each child carefully matched, and many other possibilities.

Example 6   Think of a parallel situation. Good ideas can often be stolen from elsewhere or modified to suit the particular problem concerned. In designing a better motor car one might consider other forms of transport such as boats (producing an amphibious vehicle), trains (strings of cars joined together cruising down motorways and peeling off at their appropriate exits), aircraft (helicopter blades to help evade traffic jams, aeroplane ventilation systems), submarines (periscopes make windscreens obsolete) and hovercraft (cars which float on and are surrounded by jets of air to reduce collisions).

Students facing the oral French problem might adopt ideas from other kinds of language learning, particularly first language learning, and consider oral work in the primary school especially via play (creation of language games in French), language enrichment for deprived children or language courses for immigrants (adaptation of materials produced in various national projects),[27] techniques used by speech therapists,[28] and well developed school oral arts programmes.[29]

Example 7   Chessboard. Here one must imagine a chessboard with an infinite number of squares. Along the left-hand edge each row represents ideas in one category, while along the top each column contains ideas in another category. For example, if one were devising a new kind of meal, one might list various kinds of protein food along the top – fish, pork, cheese, chicken, egg etc. – and vegetables along the side. Each square of the chessboard represents one possible combination. One thus finds commonplace combinations like fish and chips, possible but unlikely pairs such as dover sole and radishes, and unusual but intriguing dishes like sausages and globe artichokes.

The chessboard need not be two-dimensional. If further categories of ideas are nominated, multi-dimensional cells showing combinations of three or four attributes emerge. With such a structure tens of thousands of ideas are generated; most of them will be useless, but some will have both novelty and value.

Returning to our oral French idea, broad categories might

include activities for the teacher, activities for the pupil, location-timing and resources. After many a mismatch the following pro, posal could emerge. Under the headings 'location' and 'timing' a group of students will often move outside the mental set of class-room and school hours. The proposal might be to take over a nearby youth hostel for a weekend of self-catering with French assistants, college of education students, one or two teachers and a group of children. Much of the weekend will be spent playing games in French, reading French magazines, eating French food, and creating as intensive a French atmosphere as can be generated within the limitations of such a project at minimal cost to the participants. Moreover this particular proposal can easily become a reality, given the cooperation of one school.

Such productive thinking sessions are not only extremely profitable but can create very good morale among a group of students as they taste the excitement of groping for new ideas in teaching. If lifelong flexibility is increasingly to be of value to teachers, the early cultivation of mental alertness and an eye for innovation are especially healthy at the initial training stage, and, as Goldman[30] argues, divergent thinking in students ought to receive greater reward and encouragement than is often the case.

For notes to this chapter see pp 210–11.

159

6 Teaching Practice and Work with Children

Ultimately it is the larger assignments in schools, the familiar periods of teaching practice, which are likely to be valued most highly by students themselves. Yet this traditional sampling of reality often fails to provide optimum learning conditions for students. In this chapter some of the ways in which experience of working with children, both inside and outside schools, can be utilised will be examined in greater detail.

TEACHING PRACTICE

Pedley has given a cogent description of the hopes and fears which accompany the traditional teaching practice: 'We want students to acquire good, positive, optimistic attitudes (however these may be defined) from experience in good schools under the guidance of good teachers. That is, I reject what happens all too frequently now: the haphazard exposure of students to bad and mediocre schools and teachers, mainly under the pressure of the Spring Flood, when waves of students invade schools between January and March. "Sink or swim" experience is not good enough.'[1]

Cope,[2] however, has found very positive approval by students of their teaching practice experience. Over 70 per cent of the students in her sample claimed to have enjoyed it, while less than 10 per cent disliked it. In addition 95 per cent felt they had learned either a great deal or a reasonable amount from their experiences.

Cope's British enquiry has yielded useful information about the views not only of students but also of college supervisors and teachers in schools. She polled all three groups about the positive and negative aspects of teaching practice. Students derived most satisfaction from the opportunities of working with children, their membership of the school community, being able to apply ideas developed in college and sensing a growth in self-confidence and their commitment to the profession. They experienced frustration at the relative brevity of the practice and the need to accept the authority of others in the classroom, and felt anxiety about assessment of their skills. College staff valued the helping aspect of supervising students and the legitimate opportunity to work in schools, though they shared the students' reservations about brevity and lamented the inadequacy of supervisory time that was made available. Teachers welcomed the influx of new ideas and personalities in the school but sometimes resented the disruption caused. Cope concluded that teaching practice should last longer, that the tensions generated by assessment should be reduced, and that supervision should be made more constructive and meaningful.

Pedley calculates that if, as a maximum, approximately 45,000 trainees in English colleges and universities might be engaged in teaching practice at any one time, then theoretically there are six teachers per student available from whom a good supervisor might be chosen. He goes on to show, however, that the choice is not quite so wide in practice.

In fact the choice is much more restricted by several factors. These include:

(i) the need to match college output to the type of schools available locally;

(ii) the need to match students' special subjects to the specialists available in local schools;

(iii) under-use of many schools because of the haphazard geographical distribution of colleges (eg the extreme South-West has until now been relatively under-used);

(iv) many good teachers (eg Deputy Heads) are not available as supervisors because of administrative duties;

(v) not all Heads are willing to allow their schools to participate;

(vi) good teachers in bad schools must often be excluded.

The real choice is probably more like three teachers to one student (of course better than this in some areas and worse in others); and of any cross-section of three teachers, is it not true that only one is likely to be of the quality and to have the experience desired for this vitally important job?[3]

If trainees are to derive real benefits from their teaching practice experience, a number of factors must be taken into account. The James Report[4] spoke of 'school experience', a phrase open to wider interpretation than the customary 'teaching practice'. Working with children becomes for many students the most important and valuable part of the training programme, yet the very exposure of a novice to even a small number of pupils can arouse apprehension. In this chapter there will be an analysis of ways in which students can work with children in or out of schools, and a consideration of some of the problems such experiences can create.

A GENTLE INTRODUCTION

It is sometimes only with difficulty that one remembers that although student teachers may have had quite recent experience of being a pupil in a school, this does not necessarily ensure understanding of younger children nor endow them with special skills for dealing with groups. These skills have to be learned, sometimes painfully, and the argument for a gentle introduction is not a suggestion that the pain of learning should be abolished, but rather that it should be diminished to the point where the trainee is in a favourable position to derive gain from his experiences.

Otty describes the pangs of fear experienced by generations of novitiates prior to their first encounter with a full class of children:

> With a tightening of the stomach I realise that teaching practice begins very soon now. We have scarcely met any real live children. In fact only one or two short visits to a comprehensive school in the East End. My chief memory of these is of a group trooping into the school building to the cockney jeers of some second formers. One counted us off with extravagant gestures.
>
> 'Stu-dent, stu-dent, stu-dent,' and with that falling mocking cadence children use to taunt.[5]

162

One of the arguments given for the use of micro-teaching in Chapter 4 was that it broke down the formidable challenge of thirty or more children to be taught for upwards of half an hour by a lone student. Several options offer a more gentle introduction to reality.

Work with the individual child

Work with individuals is a component of almost all teaching, and in some situations may indeed be the most common mode of interaction. The teacher needs to learn several skills, some common to all one-to-one teaching, others specific and perhaps unique to a certain subject, problem or age group. Not the least of these skills is the ability simply to talk with children; and to listen, to identify difficulties, to ask questions, to respond to answers, to encourage, to urge, sometimes to restrain, always to communicate with language, gestures and other non-verbal behaviour appropriate to the particular child under the conditions operating at the time. In this sense every one-to-one interaction is unique, and yet there are communalities. Similar questions may be asked by children of the same age engaged in a common activity. Teachers learn to classify in broad terms types of problem and behaviour in children while at the same time preserving the option to make subtly different responses.

Access to individual children not only offers the student valuable experience but can also be of enormous service to schools. Given sound preparatory planning and the support of all parties concerned the following are some of the options available.

Example 1 An infants' school head in a school where many children arrive unable to talk in any comprehensible way takes twelve students to work with twelve of the most difficult cases. The children do not simply speak with a regional accent or in a slipshod way, the poorest are almost totally unable to communicate, having a small vocabulary and lacking the ability to use most basic grammatical forms such as plurals. They may rarely utter more than two words or sounds in any statement. The twelve children have been selected by the head from a combination of teachers' reports and the results of a more objective test such as the English Picture Vocabulary Test.[6] An educational psychologist or other appropriate person gives a diagnostic test such as the Illinois Test of Psycholinguistic Abilities,[7] and from the profiles obtained each student in consultation with tutor, teacher and others works out a series of activities designed to help the child reach a higher level of language performance. The gains here are manifold. The child gets a great deal of individual attention from a concerned and supportive adult; the class teacher is released to a small degree from some of the pressure to fit in time for prolonged individual attention to the neediest children; the student learns about language deprivation and enrichment, home background, learning disabilities and working with an individual child; and the school derives benefit from having extra personnel. An afternoon per week spread over a year can be extremely useful to all concerned.

Example 2 A comprehensive school has mixed ability groups for mathematics. One teacher finds that three children experience considerable difficulties, and because of the demands of the rest of the class he is not able to give as much time to explain and encourage as he would wish. Three students are used to work individually with the children and with others in classes where some pupils have difficulty with maths. The allround benefits are as described above: individual help for the child, useful assistance for the hardpressed teacher, acquisition of insights and skills for the student, and influx of extra adult personnel for the school.

Example 3 A junior school has five Chinese children, all belonging to families from Hong Kong who have come to work in Chinese restaurants. As the children are aged from seven to eleven and speak little English, the head has difficulty knowing how best to accommodate them. There are few immigrants in the school, and with such a small number and a 4 year age spread, the five hardly form a suitable teaching group. In any case it is the wish of the families that they should become integrated into appropriate classes as rapidly as possible. In association with the various class teachers five students volunteer and are assigned to a child. They help the child with ordinary school work and also

164

teach him English. Once more, as in Example 1, the commitment is perhaps an afternoon but is a regular one.

Work with individual children is extremely rewarding for students, but a certain caution must be exercised. First of all the commitment must be a guaranteed one and where possible known in advance. The child, the teacher, the head and the student all need to know that there will be four sessions, or six, or an hour once a week for a term, or an afternoon a fortnight for a whole year. This is particularly important for work with deprived or immigrant children. Furthermore the commitment must be a firm one. There is nothing more irritating for a teacher, or un-settling for a child who may have enough problems of instability in his daily life, than not to know whether or not the student will arrive. Another prerequisite is that the student should work closely with the class teacher, or what happens can either be unnecessarily duplicative or totally remote from what are known to be the needs of the child concerned.

A final important point is that for many kinds of work with individual children the students should be volunteers. It would be unfair to assign students to children from a very bad home back-ground if they are reluctant conscripts to the task. One might argue that all those who profess to be interested in a career in teaching ought to be sufficiently concerned to volunteer, and indeed many will, but reluctance to face the harsher reality of life in schools, particularly with younger students, should not be seen as either lack of motivation or cowardice. Volunteers among my own students have worked with children who came to school bruised and beaten (in one case with a child who had been sexually assaulted by his own father); have caught lice; and have been embraced by loving but nevertheless very dishevelled runny-nosed six-year-olds. This sort of work is very valuable, but for some students it is not an ideal way to make early contacts with children.

Other work with individual children might include reading practice at primary or remedial secondary levels; assisting a child with a project involving, say, photography, when a known student

165

has skill and knowledge which the class teacher does not possess; working with children who have been away from school and have fallen behind, either when these return to school and need to catch up, or, on some occasions, in homes and hospitals; or work with a very bright or musically or artistically gifted child whose skills far outstrip those of his fellows. There are endless other opportunities which can be devised by the ingenuity of teachers, tutors and students themselves in response to the overwhelming needs of children trying to learn something.

Work with groups

It was an important part of the micro-teaching format that group size should be reduced to as little as four, and indeed there are good reasons why students should encounter small groups before larger ones, both inside the college walls and in schools.

Where children are brought into college, there are numerous possibilities available, depending on the facilities at hand and the interests and needs of the students, tutors and children involved. Usually the children arrive in a state of elation, as the experience for them is partly that of a school outing, and this can be both advantageous and hazardous. It is too easy for students to devise brief bursts of apparently gripping and spectacular activity which lead nowhere and simply fill up the spaces in a superficially impressive way, though this is not entirely without use, and can lead to useful discussion and analysis sessions.

Working with groups of children inside the school, however, tends to be rather different. Here the environment is familiar to the children but strange to the students, and it is likely that the school will exert much greater control over what takes place, though schools often give students and their tutor a relatively free hand. Several possibilities present themselves in this context.

Example 1 In an open plan primary school there are four units, each consisting of two teachers and about sixty-five children. The units are divided in various ways, but the head and teaching staff would welcome extra help. Eight students spend a day every week in the school, two students to each unit. One student mans the number corner and another the language area. They do not

166

usually 'teach' in the formal sense but are available for consultation, leaving the two unit teachers free to move around other areas. Occasionally they do take a small group for some specific activity, such as storytelling, planning a project or moving to an outdoor activity. The advantages are similar to those for assigned work with individual children, that is greater freedom for the class teacher, more adult attention for children, valuable insights and experience under non-threatening conditions for students, and extra adult personnel for the school.

Example 2 A secondary school has a well planned set of activities for fifth year pupils under the Raising of the School Leaving Age programme. Unfortunately there are not enough teachers to ensure adequate help and supervision for the many small groups of pupils who will be engaged in a variety of activities, often away from the school premises. A group of students is attached to the teacher organising this elaborate programme and they are deployed with various groups both inside and outside the classroom. One of the main advantages for the students is that it gives them informal opportunities to work alongside what to them are often difficult groups of adolescents when encountered under more formal conditions and in larger numbers.

Example 3 A school has a course called 'Work and Leisure', which is a team-teaching project involving three teachers and ninety children. The course takes place every Tuesday for the whole of the morning and includes lectures, films, group discussions and visits. The three teachers would like to be able to split the large unit of ninety into twelve smaller discussion/working groups but with only three teachers this means that nine groups are without an adult supervisor at any time. Nine students join the project, watch the films, listen to the talks etc, and when smaller groups form, each student takes responsibility for one.

Example 4 Four students share the responsibility for a class under the supervision of the regular class teacher, but the latter is not necessarily present after the opening sessions. The group carries out a planned series of activities, taking it in turns to be 'lead teacher' when appropriate, especially at marshalling times. Many possibilities are available, including large group/small

167

group tasks, individual attention, remedial work, projects and integrated studies of various kinds. This and similar arrangements also release a student to observe classroom behaviour of teacher or pupils as described in Chapter 3.

In all these cases advance planning is at least as important and often essential to enable a school to build its programme of work with the guaranteed availability of a known number of students in mind.

More elaborate versions of Example 4, whereby analysis of what occurs is built into the college programme, have come to be known as study practice. Downes and Shaw[8] have described the extensive use of study practice for large numbers of students in groups of ten or twelve, each working with a tutor. The students spend half a day in school each week and subsequently another half day evaluating and planning. The analysis sessions can consist of discussion, child study and an important linking of what are generally called the theoretical parts of the course to the practical experiences gained by the participants. An additional bonus is that students who might have difficulties establishing relations and communicating with children can often be identified and helped at a relatively early stage before being exposed to the pressures of a full class, though study practice can legitimately be used at almost any stage of training, even after the more usual block practice.

BLOCK PRACTICE

One may easily caricature the block practice as an extended period of exposure to real teaching when the student, with minimal supervision, staggers blindly from one day to the next learning little other than what the passage of time might in any case have brought. This would be to malign those teachers and supervising tutors who perform a thoroughly commendable function, and to undervalue the student's ability to learn from experience even if in a random and somewhat unstructured way. What is more to the point is how, subsequent perhaps to the periods of gentle toe-dipping described above, students can gain maximum benefit

168

from teaching under conditions which are nearer to what a qualified teacher might encounter.

Traditionally block practice begins with a preliminary visit or series of visits to the school when mutual inspection by the assigned student and the head takes place, and lack of any initial hostilities signifies an unwritten contractual obligation on both sides to live with each other for the prescribed period of time. Usually at this stage the student's timetable and possibly scheme of work are devised, at best as the result of a three-way discussion involving school, student and supervising tutor. The early days of the practice usually consist of observation by the student of the teachers and classes for whom he is shortly to be responsible. This can often be an arid experience for the trainee as he rapidly sizes up existing conditions and becomes eager to take over. Finally, usually operating on a reduced timetable, he teaches normally to all external appearances a permanent member of the staff until, often to the surprise of his classes, who may have come to accept him as their teacher rather than 'the student', he reaches the end of the requisite period and returns to college. Somewhere along the line he will have been visited by one or more supervisors, probably been observed by one or more teachers in the school, and been categorised as fit or unfit to enter the profession. Countless inter-actions will have occurred. Most of them will appear to have been forgotten, many will have been filed and labelled in the student's memory and may significantly affect his future actions, and some will have left indelible scars and be recounted and analysed privately and publicly on numerous occasions.

At its worst teaching practice can become a capsule of sensory experiences floating in a vacuum, divorced from the preparatory programme, and, except for supervisors' visits, having no connection with the training institution. Afterwards some memories persist, but from the other world of institution life there is no way back. It need not be this way.

Supervision

The supervision of student teachers is a craft which most supervisors, whether they be teachers or college tutors, have learned for themselves. In itself a complexity of skills, it has tended until recently to be untaught. It remains idiosyncratic, and therein lies at once its strength and weakness, for under the blanket term 'supervision' must be included not only extremes such as non-directive counselling and ferociously autocratic tyranny, but a host of more moderate variations.

Supervision style is determined by a number of factors, but two common phenomena, both based on comparisons by the evaluator of himself with the person being judged, are worthy of consideration. First there is *compensation* – the tendency in exercising critical judgement to require the person under scrutiny to manifest a much greater amount of a quality than the observer himself possesses. If, for example, the observer subconsciously senses that he himself is untidy, badly organised and ill prepared in his own teaching, he may compensate by insisting that the student should be neat, organised and well prepared for his lessons.

The second phenomenon is that of *projection*, and this occurs when the supervisor projects himself into the place of the student, imagining how he might be reacting in a similar situation. If his self-image tends to be an exaggerated picture of what he judges to be his virtues, this sort of comparison can often be an unfair one. It is too easy to imagine oneself to be dynamic, good-humoured, tolerant, witty, sensitive, firm if necessary (but always in the kindest possible way), and repress memories of one's own sloth, intolerance, sarcasm, moodiness and insensitivity. Projection sometimes leads the supervisor to take over the lesson and test the fantasy, though there may be other reasons when this occurs. Since counselling usually involves judgement, and judgement is influenced by many factors, such as those described above, awareness of the frailty of human perception is an important quality for supervisors to possess. Abercrombie gives a crisp summary of some of the difficulties encountered.

> In receiving information from a given stimulus pattern we select from the total amount of information available (that is, from the complex of the stimulus pattern in its context) and from our own store of information. The receipt of information therefore involves making a judgment, but in many cases (as for instance in seeing

familiar things) this is done so rapidly and automatically that we are unaware of the extent of our personal involvement in the act, tending to regard the information as given. In such cases we might obtain more valid information if we could consider alternative selections from the information available.[9]

The nature of the dilemma is even more complex. Given the fragility of perception and the absence of any consensus about the qualities of good teaching, as described in Chapter 2, nevertheless the supervisor must act in some positive way, even if only to respond to the student's expectations. The student's wish is to improve his teaching. He sees the supervisor as more than a mere mirror. Depending on his own and the supervisor's personality and needs, he may see him as a director, a counsellor, a friend, a penetrating critic, a moulder, an enemy, a saboteur, an assessor, a government agent, a teacher, or even as a surgeon whose task it is to excise what is bad and repair what is broken. In the face of most of these expectations a confession of apparent total uncertainty and vagueness by the supervisor can be seen as unhelpful and lead to considerable frustration. This is not to say that certainty and precision are necessarily better. The problem is rather how to offer help and advice within the framework of limitations delineated above.

In the face of such uncertainties some supervisors opt on occasion for total non-directiveness, which in itself can cause massive anxiety. The following Becket-like conversation between a student and his bland pipe-smoking tutor reduced the former to a nervous jelly.

Student: Will you be coming pretty regularly, Mr Crawshaw?
Supervisor: (puffs pipe)
Student: I mean will it be, like, every week?
Supervisor: (long pause, continues puffing pipe)
Student: Do you usually let us know when you're coming?
Supervisor: (long pause, more pipe puffing)
Student: I mean, will you phone up or write or something?
Supervisor: (very long pause, more pipe puffing and then, in a measured voice) Basically I'm lazy.

The role of supervisor and assessor are usually combined, it being argued that those who have witnessed the student in the classroom and counselled him are in the best position to measure the quality of his teaching. There is a case for a non-assessing supervisor, that is a person of experience whose sole task is to counsel, assessment being made by others. It is not likely that students or supervisors would prefer it this way. A purely counselling supervisor could become a trusted friend, and not to solicit his comments on the student's capabilities might even do the student a disservice. Yet to solicit them would be to make him an assessor.

The status of the supervisor is of critical importance. In the student's eyes there may be a large difference between, for example, a teacher tutor only four years older than himself, a head, a young college tutor, and an elderly university professor. All these are legitimate and commonly used supervisors, some more frequently so than others. A simple statement such as 'Have you thought of splitting the group into threes for this activity?' might be interpreted as a friendly piece of advice, an order or a condemnation, depending on who uttered it.

In a brief analysis of the role of the supervisor, it is not possible to make a thorough dissection of all the relevant issues, and the strength of the idiosyncratic nature of supervision is precisely that numerous options are available and the supervisor may indeed show considerable variety in his approach to different students. What can be given is a list of some of the questions a supervisor, be he teacher, head or college/university tutor may wish to ask himself before embarking on his task.

1 How does the particular student learn and what is likely to influence him to change his behaviour? (It is assumed here that unless the student is judged to have begun his career in a state of perfection, 'learning' must be seen as changes in behaviour.)
2 What forms of feedback are already available to the student and how can I help him amplify and interpret these?
3 How certain am I when I strongly propose modifications in

what he is doing that what I suggest is (a) for the better, and (b) possible for him to accomplish?

4 How far are my perceptions influenced by a desire (a) to compensate for my own weaknesses, or (b) project my own fantasies about the kind of teacher I think I am? (To some extent compensation and projection are to be expected and are not necessarily bad. If I happen to be an untidy person, it might be a good thing that I am concerned to highlight the fault in others. One is concerned here with the *degree* to which perceptions are influenced, and the development of critical awareness of the *extent* of self-deception, where this is possible.)

5 As I am likely to be both counsellor and assessor, how far do these roles conflict? Is it possible for me to gain maximum response to my counselling function while retaining my integrity as an assessor? If the assessment function causes apprehension in students and possibly conflicts with the counselling, what steps can be taken to rectify or improve this situation?

There are endless other questions.

Apprenticeship

Stones and Morris are among several writers who have questioned the value of block practice. They describe the whole concept as being anachronistic: 'Historically the concept was based on craft apprenticeship. The pupil teacher movement had at its core the initiation of the apprentice into the mysteries of the craft by processes of telling, demonstrating and imitating. The *master* teacher told the students what to do, showed them how to do it and the students imitated the master . . . In our view the concept is now inappropriate and in need of reconsideration.'[10]

Stones and Morris do not totally reject block practice, but rather invite a reappraisal of its purpose and form. Certainly there is now a strong body of opinion that it should no longer be the *sole* practical experience, largely divorced from other elements of the training programme. Yet it remains, for the student, the closest approximation to the real job available to him, and as an integrated part of a much wider exploration of practical skills it has a very important part to play. Indeed training programmes for many jobs have an 'applications course' element to them, this being the time when what has been learned must be applied in conditions as similar to the real ones as possible. The question in other kinds of training programme is whether the novice should do the job day by day and be released say once a week and occasionally for longer periods to study it, or whether he should spend his time learning away from the job, and have regular short or long periods of exposure to work inserted in between study phases. In teacher training both options are available. Even during block practice many colleges work a 'day release' scheme whereby one day or afternoon a week is spent in the college planning and analysing the week's happenings.

Cohen and Garner in a useful students' handbook about teaching practice urge the reader to take advantage of the apprenticeship format.

> A craftsman becomes a skilled technician by the slow process of acquiring specific skills and patiently accumulating knowledge about his medium. The student, particularly while on school practice, is an apprentice to his craft, and the deliberate use of the words 'slow' and 'patiently' must indicate that the process of becoming a teacher in the real sense of the word, takes a considerable time. The student should approach this period of 'practical learning' with the spirit of the apprentice: someone who is aware of his limitations and inexperience and eager to profit and learn his craft from the advice and help of those who are already qualified.[11]

OTHER KINDS OF WORK WITH CHILDREN

Work with individual children, often with those needing special help, was described above, and Grant[12] has written about the concept of a 'social practice' in Lower Saxony, West Germany, where students spend the first of their four teaching practice blocks working with deprived children, orphans, and disturbed or delinquent children, living if necessary in the village or community where the families reside. Two similar British programmes are of interest.

174

Educational priority areas

When in 1967 the Plowden Report,[13] in an attempt to break the predictable cycle of deprivation leading to further impoverishment of the next generation, recommended that positive courses of action should be undertaken in certain areas of the country, which were to become known as Educational Priority Areas (EPA), a number of very creative and worthwhile projects arose. Among the most comprehensively documented is the Liverpool EPA project described by Midwinter.[14]

A College Tutor Liaison Group was formed and part of its function was to attach colleges to various schools to ensure a regular supply of students. The arrangement was felt to work well despite occasional setbacks. Midwinter describes the outline.

The colleges were perceptive enough to realize that we did not approach them cap-in-hand, but that we were offering a unique opportunity for engagement in a national project. We earnestly requested that, where possible, students should be deployed on a regular, intramural basis, rather than out of goodwill in free time. This was meant kindly towards the students, who the project team felt should see attachment to our work as an integral part of their course. By modifying school practice requirements and special study commitments to the realistic material of a government project, one hoped to give the students a worthwhile educative experience. In terms of the EPA dilemma, the pay-off for teacher-education could well be significant. Teacher-education is, naturally enough, a link in the cycle of events that makes the education system in a priority area what it is. Many college tutors are keen to join in with the project work in order to appreciate the more the situations for which they were preparing teachers. Few of them would perhaps have gone to the extreme where it was implied that if EPAs demanded different schools, they would require different teachers. But they took the point that colleges had a major role to play in any future development in EPA education.[15]

Hillview project

In an attempt to enable student teachers to face more effectively the challenges offered by what are commonly termed the more 'difficult' children in comprehensive schools, a number of tutors

175

at Bristol evolved a scheme, not without its difficulties and problems, whereby twelve students worked with a group of early school leavers every Wednesday afternoon throughout the year. Each student was assigned to two or three children and was responsible for their activities during the afternoon. Hannam, Smyth and Stephenson[16] have described the experiment.

Students kept journals which sometimes revealed the tensions provided on certain occasions: 'A sudden movement from Doreen caught my eye; she was standing with her back to me looking towards the assistant who was busy at the end of the shop. Her hand was quickly thrust into her blazer pocket. A feeling of panic came over me – I could not be sure she had taken anything, her actions were certainly suspicious. Vera appeared not to have noticed anything and Doreen certainly had not seen me looking. Should I have said anything to her? It was the element of doubt which held me back. I did not want to wrongly accuse her of taking anything, thus probably ruining our relationship at this early stage.'[17]

This kind of experience, whilst potentially worthwhile, puts students at considerable risk. The pressure to retain popularity, to avoid authoritarianism, clashes with the sense of social responsibility which impels the student to protect Doreen from her own waywardness. For an inexperienced person this can be quite a strain. Given good support from the school and tutors the student can learn from his own and the children's behaviour, but it is the quality and nature of the support which becomes crucial, for if the tutor or experienced teacher makes a pre-emptive bid and takes over a difficult situation, then the student is inhibited and restrained from learning for himself, but if no one interferes, the consequences of an inexperienced person's errors of judgement might be serious.

Sheldart

It was with students' freedom of choice in mind that the Exeter University Sheldart project was designed. The formula has but small similarities to the projects described above.

Since, in conventional school practice, students have only

limited freedom to operate as they wish, possibly for the best of reasons, ie protection of the long-term welfare and interests of the children they teach, it was decided at Exeter University Department of Education that two tutors, twelve students, a teacher and twenty-four children should live for 2 weeks in a residential hostel on Dartmoor. The students should be responsible for the programme, but the teacher and tutors would be there as human resources, counsellors, facilitators and, if necessary, safety officers. The formula varied, in that it could well be one tutor and eight students and far less than 2 weeks, but it usually followed a grand micro-teaching format. The first week saw one group of twenty-four children, and, after a weekend of reflection, analysis and planning, the arrival of a second group for another week. As the students were all graduates, it was for many their first contact with this kind of situation, and indeed it took place before the training course.

The details, in essence, are as described, but to give a little of the flavour of the programme a diary of the first week may be of interest. The names of the centre and the people are all fictitious. The events are real, though they represent only a fraction of what happened in such a week.

SHELDART PROJECT DIARY

Friday afternoon A group which has never met before assembles at the Sheldart Centre. There are four men and four women students, and Graham Fowler, the tutor, who devised the residential centre idea and is strongly committed to it. The eight students have all volunteered to take part in the 2 week project with twenty-four children who are due to arrive on Monday morning. The task over the weekend is to plan a programme of activities. After a friendly but slightly uneasy evening meal Graham Fowler collects the eight students together and explains that although he is available as a resource, it is not his role to direct the activities. He will leave the group to have its first meeting while he clears away after the evening meal. They are to have preliminary discussions and he will rejoin them after an hour. A

177

painful vacuum is created by his departure. There has been little time to evaluate the possibilities of the lovely converted farm which constitutes the Sheldart Centre, and as the group has never met, no obvious leaders have yet emerged. Jim assumes command and launches into a plan he had prepared at home. The children will be divided into four groups of six, the first day will have four programmes each run by two students, and all children will rotate around the activities on successive days until every child has sampled every programme. Sally, whose father teaches at a well known progressive school, instinctively raises the question of choice. Are the children to be assigned or may they choose not to participate? Jim is thrown by the question as his scheme had a certain administrative tidiness which choice threatens to distintegrate. Tom, a biologist, is less concerned about frameworks as he is perfectly clear that his own contribution is to be a nature trail which he will arrange a day in advance. Meanwhile Ann is eagerly writing down the ideas which emerge from discussion and argument. When Graham Fowler returns after one hour, Donald has said little and Mike, Paula and Jane have not uttered a single word. Graham Fowler tries to draw the group back to asking what a group of children might usefully do for a week. Tom wishes to know if it has to be something educational, but there follows an inconclusive discussion about what is and is not held to be 'educational' by different people. By nightfall interesting issues have been raised but so far no details of any programme.

Saturday The morning discussion begins with Tom asking for ideas which Ann is to note down. As they do not yet know each other well enough, people should offer activities they would be willing to organise or initiate and then selections can be made. Donald makes his maiden speech and volunteers to organise singing round a camp-fire one evening. Paula breaks her silence by informing the group that she has had experience of camping with the girl guides. This is greeted by an insensitive guffaw from Jim, who appears not to notice Paula's embarrassed reaction. She is not likely to make another contribution for some time. In the afternoon the eight students explore the centre and the immediate surroundings so they will be better informed at the evening session,

178

which is much more relaxed, even euphoric on occasion. Graham Fowler plays little part in the discussion and often leaves the group to contrive its planning alone. Midway through the evening he finds Jane, who has still not said a word, in tears. She has withdrawn from the group and he fears that Jim may have said something to offend her. This is not the case, however. What upsets her, she says, is the rest of the group's enthusiasm and volume of good ideas. She has had doubts about her ability to teach, she reveals, and for her this fortnight will show whether these doubts are justified. She feels petrified at the thought of twenty-four children descending in 2 days time. She knows she has nothing to offer. Graham Fowler points out that it is likely that most if not all the members of the group are feeling apprehensive, though they may conceal it with great skill or manifest it in other ways. This reassures her sufficiently to enable her to resume her place at the meeting, though the others sense that she is distressed. Sally in particular shows great kindness to her subsequently. After the meeting one or two go to bed but most sit and listen to records. Tom laughingly suggests that they can do this every evening when the children are asleep, which prompts Ann to ask what time they will be required to go to bed. Sally questions the right of anyone to determine someone else's sleeping habits and gains some support for an open policy of going to sleep when one is tired. Eventually after a vigorous statement from Ann that children will tire themselves and perhaps even become ill, it is agreed that a firm suggestion of bed at 9.30 and lights out at 10 pm will operate, but that the children rather than the students should be responsible for regulating this arrangement.

Sunday A reminder from Graham Fowler that Eva Gregg, the teacher who is to accompany the children, will attend the afternoon meeting to find out what has emerged so far creates a sense of urgency. Jim suggests writing the skeleton week's programme on a blackboard so that Eva Gregg can see at a glance what has been planned. Ann draws up the outline, and Donald observes that although Monday and Tuesday are full to capacity, Wednesday and Thursday are thinly provided. Jim, with retrospective wisdom, decides that this is tactically a good idea, as

179

both children and students will be in a better position to devise options after the first 2 days' experiences have been evaluated. Sally insists that to date it has scarcely been suggested that children will have the opportunity to initiate. It has been assumed, she points out, that children will simply choose one of three possible options each morning, afternoon or evening. Even the choice to do none of the designated activities has not been allowed for, let alone machinery for children to initiate been devised. Mike breaks an almost total 2 day silence by apologising for raising a mundane matter, and enquiring what is to happen when the bus arrives. This intervention is met by stupefied silence. Mike persists. Elaborate plans have been made but no one has yet said what is to happen when the bus arrives and twenty-four energetic children emerge. Sally offers to make drinks for them all after they have unpacked and found themselves a bunk. The rest of the morning is to consist of a conducted tour of the Centre's grounds and buildings followed by volleyball for those who wish. Eva Gregg arrives and offers to provide equipment and materials from school if these are needed. She tells of the idiosyncracies of members of the group of twelve-year-olds, many of whom have never stayed away from home before. Two in particular may cause difficulties. There is Barry, a withdrawn boy with few friends who has run away from school and home, and might, if upset, run away from the Centre, and also Clive, who has a history of minor violence and bullying. The atmosphere becomes rather more tense and Graham Fowler reminds the group that although his interventions will be minimal, he and Eva would immediately assume responsibility if children's welfare or safety were at stake and students were not able to cope with incidents that arose.

Monday As breakfast is cleared away, Ann asks innocently who will be responsible for administering lunch arrangements such as cooking and washing up. Although it had been agreed much earlier that a rota of children and students would operate, the actual assignment of names has not been made. Ann and Tom rapidly draw up a list. Graham Fowler is relieved, as he would have needed to intervene to prevent the first meal being a fiasco had Ann not raised the issue. When the bus appears, Jim im-

180

mediately leaps aboard to welcome everyone to Sheldart. Sally, Ann and Tom talk readily to the children, while Paula and Jane quietly make and serve the drinks which Sally had volunteered to do but forgotten in the excitement. Donald stands and watches apprehensively and Mike grins shyly from behind his orange juice. Volleyball proves an effective leveller and provides a great deal of somewhat nervous jocularity and banter from participating students, usually at the expense of each other, to the slight mystification of the children taking part. Afternoon activities, which include Tom's nature trail, a visit to a nearby castle and clay modelling, appear to be very successful. All the children take part except two of the girls, who stay in making blackberry crumble. There is a self-congratulatory glow at tea time which persists until Jim reminds Sally that she is responsible for the evening programme, which, according to the chart, is to consist of drama and games in the barn. The so-called drama session is a catastrophe. Sally has little idea what to do with twenty-four lively children and after a 10 minute attempt to get groups of four to improvise a scene, finds that most of the children have completely lost interest. Some of the boys are wrestling on the floor and only Tom picks up the courage to intervene and risk the popularity which the rest are so eager to maintain. Jim hopefully puts on records and suggests dancing, but apart from four girls no one else joins in. At the analysis session after the children are in bed Sally is bitterly apologetic about what she calls her 'flop'. Graham Fowler suggests they should analyse the day as objectively as possible, and, rather than assign blame, look constructively at the following day's activities in the light of the first day's experiences. He reminds them that several things went well. In the distance noisy celebrations are heard from the boys' dormitory at 11 o'clock, and the faint, somewhat cracked voice of Tom issuing his third 'final warning' that they should now go to sleep produces nervous laughter from the other tired students.

Tuesday Volleyball is really popular, and with the most unlikely people. Already there is talk of a league and challenge matches, but on the whole informal games occur when sufficient people are inclined to play. Jim and a group are off to the sea for

181

the day taking a packed lunch. Ann enquires innocently if the trip is in any sense educational, and Jim replies that mere exposure to himself for the day will be an education for the children. The two girls again opt to make blackberry crumble all afternoon. Most of the rest play a very elaborate and greatly enjoyed wide game devised by Tom and the more passive Jane. During a lull before tea Clive, one of the 'difficult' boys, is seen playing a game of his own devising whereby he hits stones with a cricket bat in the direction of people passing by. Mike, Donald, Paula and Sally all walk by head down pretending they have not noticed. Graham Fowler has to take Clive aside and dissuade him. A 'games in the barn' session is slightly more successful than the previous evening, but one event goes well when Jim has everyone moving to a record and freezing when the music stops. In effect it becomes like dancing except that this time everyone has joined in. At the analysis session Graham Fowler raises the question of organisation, which he feels is good during the day but poor in the evenings, and, a more difficult point, the embarrassed ignoring of Clive's dangerous behaviour by those who saw it.

Wednesday The weather is very fine and without warning Jim begins to ask who might like to camp out on the nearby moor. To his delight half the girls and almost all the boys volunteer. Sadly Jim has no idea what this is going to involve and Graham Fowler and Eva Gregg work energetically, with Paula's assistance, to prepare equipment and food. Jim realises that his instant inspiration involves a colossal amount of work and belatedly joins in. By late afternoon the campers are on their way and the evening passes quietly.

Thursday In many ways the most successful day of the week. All day-to-day operations such as cooking, cleaning etc go smoothly and there is a very relaxed, warm feeling among both children and students. Jane has spent a great deal of time with Barry, who has caused no trouble whatsoever and been quite at ease. The evening camp-fire sees Donald in action for the first time for a rather flat sing-song. Most of the day children have made masks for the camp-fire or rehearsed acts for a hilarious talent show in which Mike appears with unexpected gusto.

Friday   Genuine sadness on all sides as the children pack up and leave. Saturday will be a rest day, but first the week must be analysed and buried so that all will be fresh on Sunday to plan the second week with a new group of children. Graham Fowler makes few contributions as the participants are both weary and well aware of many of the deficiencies of the first week.

Evaluation Session   Some three weeks after the fortnight has been completed the eight students assemble at Graham Fowler's house to talk through their communal experiences. They have since visited the school and been disappointed at what they saw. The children were in uniforms and appeared a little shy at meeting in this different context, though many were just as friendly as they had been at Sheldart. All students felt the two weeks were worthwhile from their point of view. They were all good friends, had learned many things about the children and themselves. Mike described it as the happiest fortnight of his life, which told people something about his life to date.

Graham Fowler was left with a host of questions. Should he have played a more dominant role as tutor? The group reported that they were surprised he did not initiate more himself even though they accepted that it was to be their programme. After all, Sally observed, he is an experienced drama teacher and she would have welcomed being able to see a good drama session after her own failure. Should he have urged the quieter members to participate more? Most initiatives came from Tom, Jim or Sally. Ann, Jane and Paula were thoroughly reliable but usually got on quietly with what others had initiated. Mike had grinned his way amiably through the fortnight but done little, and Donald had been almost a complete passenger. Why had the students volunteered? Some were simply attracted by a residential group activity involving students and children. Others, like Jane and Mike, were terrified of teaching practice and saw this as a gentle informal introduction to working with children. Is the situation unreal? After all there are many more constraints in schools than out at a self-contained Centre. Hence the students' disappointment when they saw the children later in formal surroundings. Perhaps it might be better if students worked in the school first and then

183

had the residential experience. On some issues there was little doubt. The students were very positive in their evaluation of it as a most useful insight into the problems of discipline, human relationships, curriculum, management and organisation. The children were also positive in their approval, even when things, as the students saw it, had gone 'wrong'. From the students' point of view, too, there was no other group they would know as well as this one with whom they had lived for two weeks. At the end of the whole course all the students rated it as an experience as valuable as their block practice. Sadly Donald proved as inept in school as he had been at Sheldart and failed teaching practice. He was subsequently re-examined, however, and finally obtained his teaching certificate. Jane, who had had such severe doubts at the outset, thoroughly enjoyed the course. Mike struggled through, smiling benignly when difficulties arose, as these did more noticeably in his first year of teaching. Jim's final comment was that he never realised his effect on a group of colleagues until for once he got to know one group well enough for them to be able to tell him.

For notes to this chapter see p 212.

7 Resources

I once went to watch a student teach a difficult third year class. It was a French lesson which was to take place in an old hut erected temporarily in 1918. The room 'blackout' consisted of assorted pieces of cardboard which, at intervals, fell on the heads of children sitting underneath as heavy lorries thundered past on the main road outside. The student was looking apprehensively at the tape recorder, a pre rev-counter model with little pieces of white paper marking key places on the tape. As she was about to pluck up sufficient courage to set the audio-visual unit in motion, the bulb in the projector failed noisily to the vast amusement of the class. The tape recorder obstinately refused, first to disgorge any sound, and finally to rotate at all. Just when we were all firmly convinced no further disaster was possible, the class's regular teacher appeared and delivered a staccato warning that they should all behave today as the man at the back was a tutor who had come to see if Miss — could teach. My heart bled for her, and together we improvised a barely adequate salvage operation.

My mind went back to the time when a group of students watching a videotape on teaching strategies which I had prepared with loving care were surprised to see a four-minute insert consisting of children pulling hideous faces at the camera. A well meaning technician had been demonstrating the equipment to them and made a recording on the wrong tape. My reaction scarcely supported McLuhan's description of television as a 'cool' medium. On another occasion a group of thirty students sat with pens poised, eagerly waiting to code a sound tape of a lesson during interaction analysis training. An unscheduled power cut after less than 30 seconds left us all staring impotently at a loop of limp brown tape dangling uselessly over the edge of the table. The feeling is akin to that of Woody Allen, the American writer and film actor, who claims that when he travels in a lift it takes him down to the basement and beats him up.

In the wake of such public defeats, however, when the pressure is to return to the single resource known to have limitations yet reliability, namely oneself, aided by a piece of white chalk and a loud voice, why do we persist in amplifying our teaching with resources which sometimes defy control? Many of the arguments for resource-based learning in schools, eloquently stated by Taylor,[1] hold equal validity in a teacher training context: that it permits a more active and personal involvement, that the pace can be more suited to the individual and that several different sources of information can be made available to the learner, not merely the personal views of his teacher.

Several of the ideas described in earlier parts of this book presuppose that the tutor will be willing to create or provide certain resources. Packaged materials, videotapes, film, tapes, and tape/slide presentations can all be designed with a known group of students in view. For some of the materials there would be wider than local use, and Taylor's description of the functions of a 'cooperative' are again valid: members can meet to design and exchange materials, tutors may be seconded to create resources, and pooled accounts of the response of students to the materials may enable the latter to be modified and improved more effectively than might otherwise be the case.

Equally important is the breadth of options available when a rich variety of resources is to hand: students can belong to a group with a tutor within varying degrees of structure; they can work in a group without a tutor, though probably with his guidance, and explore; and they can sometimes learn alone or with a chosen companion. In teacher training we are open to be judged by the standards we set for our students, and nothing irritates them more than being subjected to constant pontification on variety, creativity, flexibility, child-centredness and enthusiasm by someone whose very aridity and lack of these qualities suggests that he has only read about them.

It is not the purpose of this chapter to give minute technical details of each type of resource under consideration. There are many other sources which do this thoroughly. Nor is it proposed that the huge range of possibilities should be covered. The uses of various media are fully explored in books such as that by Wittich and Schuller.[2] It is, however, worthwhile to examine some of the more commonly used resources in greater detail.

MATERIAL RESOURCES

Packaged materials

These are most likely to be used in conjunction with simulation techniques, as described in Chapter 5, though they will have other uses in self-contained micro-teaching and interaction analysis packs or as supplementary material in other contexts, such as the tape/slide sequences described below.

There is little to say about these except that the reprographic standard should be as high as possible. If there are case study materials in a wallet, for example, and these include such items as letters and reports, realism can be obtained by photo-copying techniques. Anything of a textual nature should also be produced to as high a standard as possible.

The establishment of a resources unit, with offset litho, photo-copying facilities, a technician, a graphics specialist and a wide range of modern equipment, is almost a prerequisite if good quality materials tailored to local needs are required. Such a unit can either be based in a single institution or within a co-operative.

Tape/slide sequences

These can be useful, with or without additional documentation, for either group or individual work. A sequence of colour slides is taken and a sound commentary on tape is added. The sound tape can be pulsed so that, in conjunction with a tape/slide synchroniser unit, the sequence will run without a manual operator.

An example of one of the tape/slide sequences I have developed will illustrate the general principles. It is on the theme of teaching

187

in an open-plan primary school. The sound tape is of myself and the headmaster of an open-plan school discussing the buildings, the teacher and the child.

Pictures 1–4 Plans of various open-plan schools showing home bases, quiet areas, maths corners, hall and circulation space. Discussion on tape of variety of building patterns labelled 'open-plan' and purposes of such schools.

Pictures 5–10 Photographs of building features such as sliding doors and screens, as well as some of the features seen on plans in the first four pictures. Discussion of how an architect can design to suit the needs of the teacher and children. Features which teachers do not like are shown as well as those with which they are pleased.

Pictures 11–20 Discussion about the teacher covers such topics as the teacher's role in team teaching, the use of specialist areas for music, art and craft, number, reading and language skills development. The pictures show teachers and children at work in different parts of open plan units.

Pictures 21–30 Discussion concentrates on the child in the open-plan school, the question of pastoral care, recording of his progress, the qualities he needs to develop to learn in this environment and the requirements of younger and older children. Pictures show more children at work on a variety of activities.

Many other possibilities for tape/slide sequences present themselves: types of school, including pictures of unusual or intriguing schools, layout of classrooms or specialist areas such as laboratories or art rooms, grouping of children in informal and formal classrooms, wall and other display areas; there is no end to the possibilities. Taped commentaries, with or without an accompanying booklet, worksheet or assignment, can often incorporate the contributions of the teachers or children shown in the pictures.

Time-lapse photography

This technique is related to the methods used in tape/slide sequences but contains quite different elements. Time-lapse photography has been used extensively to show speeded-up versions of events which could not normally be viewed in their complete form because they are spread over too long a period. A common example is the growth of an organism or a flower bursting into bloom. By showing at speed single pictures taken at perhaps 20 or 30 minute intervals, the slowly occurring events of weeks or months can be witnessed in minutes or even seconds.

Time-lapse photographic records of classrooms were pioneered by Walker and Adelman at Chelsea College, London. A 16 mm camera is used to take pictures, at intervals of anything from half a second up to 2-3 seconds, of a class or group of children at work or at play. At the same time a record of sound is made on tape, possibly with the teacher wearing a radio microphone. When the film has been processed, it can be projected with the sound tape, and the effect is of a jerky but realistic record of what took place. Single frames can be studied in detail and 35 mm enlargements made of the more interesting shots. The technique is particularly valuable for showing general movement as well as particular gestures that may be of importance. The cost is less than that of videotape or normal cine-film, and gives a permanent record which can be analysed and discussed in numerous ways.

As the technique is at a comparatively early stage of development, the full range of possibilities in teacher training is not yet known, but there is considerable room for development and exploration. The mechanics of the operation are described in greater detail by Moreman.[3]

Film

One needs to distinguish between commercially produced and home-made film. The former is usually of a high standard technically, but may offer little to a particular institution. Too frequently one knows nothing or very little about the background of the film before ordering, and indeed one of the problems of sending for even popular and useful films is that one often has to instruct the audience that certain sections are irrelevant to their immediate needs, or outside the focus of their present scrutiny, and should be ignored. Nevertheless there are many excellent films available and they can be used with great benefit.

Chubb[4] has outlined the advantages of film as giving a permanent image in colour or black and white, enlarging specific detail and bringing it to the attention of the audience, offering live sound or commentary or both, using sound effects and music if necessary to enhance realism and create mood, and enabling the editor to achieve changes of viewpoint, scale or location almost at will. Groves[5] has collected together a series of articles on the use of film in higher education, and the contributions by Duncan[6] on the role of the producer, Lucey[7] on the cost of film-making, and Gardener,[8] who gives useful advice to the novice film-maker, are of special value to those contemplating establishing a film unit. Once again, in view of the cost in money and personnel time involved in film-making, the greatest benefit could be secured via a cooperative resource-pooling enterprise.

The section on videotapes below will contain some points of interest to the film-maker, as there is a great deal of common ground.

Sound and videotape

Television equipment is of enormous value in teacher training. It can be used for assembling filmed material showing teaching styles and classroom events for study or discussion, as well as being a valuable source of feedback in micro-teaching. It has the advantage over film of offering instant playback instead of a long wait for processing, which is essential in behaviour-changing exercises, and tapes can be wiped when no longer needed. Sound tapes can sometimes be used as a cheaper substitute – for example, when lesson dialogue is to be analysed – but usually the vastly fuller record offered by videotape seems worth the extra initial expense.

Following a conference in Turin in July 1972 the UNESCO Division of Methods, Materials and Techniques suggested four equipment modules designed to suit the needs of teacher training establishments.[9]

Module I Transmission unit A basic simple unit to which further equipment can be added at a later date, it consists of a classroom where nationally produced TV programmes can be viewed. The addition of a VTR (videotape recorder) enables off-air recording from national TV networks, as well as playback of videotapes recorded locally or by a cooperating college. The VTR can either be reel-to-reel or cassette, fixed or mobile. In a classroom of around 700 sq ft two 23 in monitors are needed, and these should be placed down the same side of the room suitably angled to give maximum visibility. It is suggested that viewers should be able to sit not nearer than 6 and not further than 20 ft from one of the monitors.

If necessary a suite of classrooms can be equipped to receive video transmissions, though this will clearly increase the cost substantially. For 150 students one set of mains and battery-operated equipment is recommended. Mains equipment consists of camera, VTR, gun microphone fixed to camera, two hyper-cardioid microphones, one neck microphone, stands, 800W quartz-iodine lamp, sound mixer, other small accessories, and fifty videotapes. Portable equipment similar to the equipment described above would be a little cheaper.

Module II   Observation unit   This consists mainly of a camera and VTR for film-making and micro-teaching. The planning is based on 100–150 students or other users. Two such modules would be needed for a simple micro-teaching programme. Module II can complement some version of Module I, thus giving both recording and mass playback options. The equipment can either use mains voltage or be independently battery-operated.

For 150 students one set of mains and battery-operated equipment is recommended. Mains equipment consists of camera, VTR, gun microphone fixed to camera, two hypercardioid microphones, one neck microphone, stands, 800W quartz iodine lamp, sound mixer and other small accessories, and fifty videotapes.

Making films or sound tapes in classrooms, even where these are specially built, presents recording problems. Use of correctly positioned and installed hypercardioid microphones, though expensive, is very effective. Similarly the mounting of a very directional gun microphone on the camera gives a good quality realistic record of the speaker being filmed, though care must be taken that camera noise is not picked up. In micro-teaching a neck microphone can be used, and if necessary placed on a table

191

at the front of the class. A sound mixer is necessary to enable a balance to be achieved between the usually louder teacher's voice and the less audible pupils' voices. The gun microphone will normally cut down background noise when filming takes place outdoors or in a noisy classroom.

Module III   Reporting and production studio   This is a more elaborate recording studio, usually requiring a full-time administrator or supervising tutor, such as might be found in a large institution or a cooperative serving a number of smaller colleges. As such it represents an extension of the facilities described in Modules I and II. The installation includes a control room attached to a specially equipped studio/observation classroom. There are three cameras, one of which is remote controlled, four hypercardioid microphones and one gun microphone, four monitors (a 9 in monitor for each camera and a 17 in line control monitor), image and audio mixers (which include special effects generator, camera mixer and intercom), and several items of auxillary equipment such as quartz iodine lighting, telescopic stands etc. Where Module III serves a cooperative both 1 in and $\frac{1}{2}$ in videotape recorders should be installed.

A second version of Module III is the mobile version, which can either be portable equipment to be installed in a classroom elsewhere or fixed inside a vehicle. In the latter case the vehicle would house all sound and image equipment and controls, as well as a set of rollers for camera cables and microphones. The cameras, microphones and lighting would be transported to the classroom where actual filming was to take place. The vehicle might be equipped with its own generator, rendering it independent of mains power sources.

Module III is essential where 'split-screen' or other effects are desired (as described in Chapter 4), where high quality films are to be made, or where tapes from outside institutions are to be copied or modified. It must also be emphasised that this module cannot be operated effectively without both a full-time technician and supervising tutor.

Module IV   A production centre   This is a more elaborate version of Module III and would normally only be considered on a

192

national or regional scale, probably linked to large colleges, universities or development centres. There would need to be a team of research and development personnel and several technicians. No further details are given, as these would obviously vary from country to country and region to region, but there would be substantial initial capital expenditure, and annual salaries, maintenance and replacement costs would also be very large. Appendix B gives an estimate of the cost of this and other modules.

HUMAN RESOURCES

It is no reflection on the relative importance of human resources that most of this chapter, and indeed of the whole book, should concern itself with techniques, materials and equipment, and little be devoted to the people who develop and apply them. A different kind of book would concentrate largely on the personal qualities of the teacher trainer, but it is taken for granted here that those who take the trouble to inform themselves about recent developments will wish to apply them with the zeal, intelligence and understanding they require. This is perhaps too big an assumption, but without the warmth of human sensitivity techniques are arid and materials a collection of expensive baubles. To expect that the introduction of micro-teaching, interaction analysis, role-playing or simulation will of themselves vastly improve the quality of teaching, both within the institution and of the students being trained, would be akin to hoping that birthday toys would make an unhappy child contented, irrespective of the relationships within his family.

ENDNOTE

Peck and Tucker[10] end their 1973 summary of research on teacher education with a more optimistic appraisal of current practice than that of Ned Flanders in 1963 cited at the beginning of this book.

Just within the past 10 to 15 years the operational skills of teaching have become better defined and measured than ever before. Traditional teacher education, with its frequently lengthy stays in the semantic stratosphere, has not done a very effective job of developing these skills, particularly at the pre-service level. Accumulating evidence does suggest, however, that a genuine revolution in the nature and quality of teacher education is already visible on the horizon . . .

At the pre-service level, well-planned, early involvement in actual teaching seems likely to be available to more and more students. The influence of the most widely favoured systems for conceptualising effective teaching, and the emergence of more effective techniques for training teachers in this direction, both seem likely to accelerate the move toward more active, self-directed learning, both for teachers and for their pupils.

Meanwhile, skilled manpower and improved technology are becoming available on an increasing scale, to make possible more penetrating and more adequately comprehensive studies of alternative training procedures.

If imaginative and innovative developments continue to emerge as readily as was the case in the decade from 1963 to 1973 then such optimism is well justified.

For notes to this chapter see pp 212–13.

Notes and References

Preface (*pages* vii–xiii)

1 Flanders, N. A. 'Intent, Action and Feedback: A Preparation for Teaching', *Journal of Teacher Education*, 14 (1963), 251–60
2 Duthie, J. H. *Primary School Survey* (Edinburgh, 1970)
3 Hilsum, S. and Cane, B. S. *The Teacher's Day* (NFER, Slough, 1971)
4 Ibid, 220

1: Some Historical Exemplars (*pages* 15–43)

1 Church, Dean. *The Oxford Movement*. Quoted in G. Ogren. *Trends in English Teacher Training from 1800* (Stockholm, 1953), 10
2 Fuller, F. *The Founding of St Luke's College Exeter* (*1839–1864*) (Exeter, 1966), 42
3 National Society Report (May 1840). Quoted by Fuller, op cit, 46
4 Seaborne, M. *A Visual History of Modern Britain – Education* (1966), 70
5 Okafor-Omali, D. *A Nigerian Villager in Two Worlds* (1965), 51
6 Smith, F. *A History of English Elementary Education 1760–1902* (1931), 37
7 Baring-Gould, S. *The Vicar of Morgenstow*. Quoted by Fuller, op cit, 15–16
8 Broudy, H. S. 'Historic Exemplars of Teaching Method', in N. L. Gage (ed). *Handbook of Research on Teaching* (Chicago, 1963), 3–4

9   Holmes, B. 'Teacher Education in a Changing World', in G. Z. F. Bereday and J. A. Lauwerys. *The Education and Training of Teachers* (1963), 5

10 Richardson, T. A. 'The Classical Chinese Teacher', in Bereday and Lauwerys, op cit, 30

11 Ibid, 27

12 Price, R. F. *Education in Communist China* (1970), 222

13 Howie, G. 'The Teacher in Classical Greece and Rome', in Bereday and Lauwerys, op cit, 43

14 Broudy, op cit, 6

15 Horace. *Satires* i, 6, 81–82. Quoted in Howie, op cit, 51

16 Seneca. *Epistles* 106, 12. Quoted in Howie, op cit, 56

17 Rich, R. W. *The Training of Teachers in England and Wales during the Nineteenth Century* (Cambridge, 1933), 22

18 Fitzpatrick, E. A. *St Ignatius and the Ratio Studiorum* (New York, 1933), 212–13. Quoted in Broudy, op cit, 22–3

19 Smith, op cit, 71

20 Seaborne, op cit, plate 110

21 Dent, H. C. 'An Historical Perspective', in S. Hewett (ed). *The Training of Teachers* (1971), 12

22 Southey, R. and C. C. *Life of Rev. Andrew Bell* (1844). Quoted in Rich, op cit, 4

23 Rich, op cit, 11

24 1807, Parliamentary Debates. Quoted in Ogren, op cit, 25

25 Binns, H. C. *A Century of Education* (1908), 79

26 Cross Commission, 1888. Quoted in Ogren, op cit, 28–9

27 Rich, op cit, 78

28 Cruickshank, M. 'David Stow, Scottish Pioneer of Teacher Training in Britain', *British Journal of Educational Studies*, XIV, 2, 205

29 Stow, D. *The Training System, Moral Training School and Normal Seminary or College* (Glasgow, 1836), 26

30 Jeffreys, M. V. C. *Revolution in Teacher-Training* (1961), 3

31 Thabault, R. 'The Professional Training of Teachers in France', in Bereday and Lauwerys, op cit, 244–55

32 Messerli, J. C. 'Horace Mann and Teacher Education', in Bereday and Lauwerys, op cit, 70–84

33 Elsbree, W. S. 'Teacher Education in the United States', in Bereday and Lauwerys, op cit, 177-91
34 Ogren, op cit, 132-3
35 Fuller, op cit, 160
36 Ibid, 182
37 Annual Report of the Exeter Diocesan Board of Education (1849), 6
38 Taylor, W. *Society and the Education of Teachers* (1969), 97
39 Fuller, op cit, 178
40 Ibid, 177
41 Taylor, op cit, 95
42 Ibid, 95
43 Newcastle Commission 1861, 270
44 Dickens, Charles. *Hard Times* (1854). Quoted in A. Tropp. *The School Teachers* (1957), 24
45 Rugg, H. *The Teacher of Teachers* (New York, 1952), 37
46 Dent, op cit, 22
47 National Education Association. *Addresses and Proceedings* (1907), 537

2: *The Student Teacher* (*pages* 44-70)

1 Evans, K. M. 'An Annotated Bibliography of British Research on Teaching and Teacher Ability', *Educational Research*, 4, 1 (1961), 67-80
2 Allen, E. A. 'The Professional Training of Teachers', *Educational Research*, 5, 3 (1963), 200-15
3 Cane, B. 'Teachers, Teaching and Teacher Education', in H. J. Butcher. *Educational Research in Britain* (1968), 314-31
4 Taylor, W. *Towards a Policy for the Education of Teachers*, Colston Papers no 20 (1969)
5 Cope, E. 'Teacher Training and School Practice', *Educational Research*, 12, 2 (1970), 87-98
6 Cane, op cit, 314
7 Taylor, *Towards a Policy* ..., op cit, 223
8 University of Toledo, Ohio, Research Foundation. *The*

Characteristics of Teacher Education Students in the British Isles and the United States (1965)

9   Evans, E. G. S. 'Reasoning Ability and Personality Differences amongst Student Teachers', *British Journal of Educational Psychology*, 34 (1964), 305–14

10 Floud J. E. and Scott W. 'Recruitment to Teaching in England and Wales', in J. E. Floud, A. H. Halsey and C. A. Anderson. *Education, Economy and Society* (New York, 1961)

11 Robbins Report (1964)

12 Ashley, B., Cohen H. and Slatter, R. 'Social Classifications: Relevance to the Teacher', *Times Educational Supplement* (17 March 1967)

13 Isaac, J. 'Social Origins of Trainee Teachers', *Higher Educational Journal*, 17, 3 (1969)

14 Wright, B. D. and Tuska, S. A. *From Dream to Life in the Psychology of Becoming a Teacher* (Chicago, 1966)

15 Altman, E. 'The Mature Student Teacher', *New Society* (28 December 1967)

16 Valentine, C. W. 'Reasons for the Choice of the Teaching Profession by University Students', *British Journal of Educational Psychology*, 4 (1934), 237–58

17 Tudhope, W. B. 'Motives for the Choice of the Teaching Profession by Training College Students', *British Journal of Educational Psychology*, 14 (1944), 129–41

18 Wragg, E. C. 'Attitudes, Anxieties and Aspirations of Graduates Following the Postgraduate Certificate of Education'. Unpublished MEd Thesis, Leicester University (1967)

19 Veness, T. *School Leavers, Their Aspirations and Expectations* (1962)

20 Pinsent, A. 'Pre-college Teaching Experience and Other Factors in the Teaching Success of University Students', *British Journal of Educational Psychology*, 3 (1933), 109–25 and 201–20

21 Turnbull, G. H. 'The Influence of Previous Teaching Experience on Results Obtained by Students in a University

Department of Education', *British Journal of Educational Psychology*, 4 (1934), 1–9

22 Saer, H. 'A Further Investigation of Pre-college Teaching Experiences and Other Factors in the Teaching Success of University Students', *British Journal of Educational Psychology*, 11 (1941), 183–96

23 Lawton, J. R. 'A Study of Factors Useful in Choosing Candidates for the Teaching Profession', *British Journal of Educational Psychology*, 9, 2 (1939), 131–44

24 Phillips, A. S. 'An Examination of Methods of Selection of Training College Students'. Unpublished MA Thesis, London University (1953)

25 Burroughs, G. E. R. 'A Study of the Interview in the Selection of Students for Teacher Training', *British Journal of Educational Psychology*, 28 (1958), 37–46

26 Lovell, K. 'An Investigation into Factors Underlying Teaching Ability'. Unpublished MA Thesis, London University (1951)

27 Burroughs, op cit, 37

28 Halliwell, K. 'An Investigation into the Selection of Students Admitted to a Teachers' Training College'. Unpublished PhD Thesis, Sheffield University (1965)

29 Allen, M. 'A Comparison Between Group and Individual Selection Procedures in a Training College'. Unpublished MEd Thesis, Manchester University (1962)

30 Tarpey, M. S. 'Personality Factors in Teacher Trainee Selection', *British Journal of Educational Psychology*, 35 (1965), 140–49

31 Grant, J. J. 'A "Social Practice" in the Training of Teachers: A West German Model', *Education for Teaching* (Autumn 1967), 19–24

32 Floud, J. 'Teaching in the Affluent Society', in Bereday and Lauwreys, op cit, 387

33 Hannam, C. C., Smyth P., Stephenson, N. 'Supplementing Teacher Practice: The Student and the Small Group', *Education for Teaching* (February 1967), 68–74

34 Thymme-Gouda, T. V. 'A Study of the Attitudes of Teachers

in England towards their Courses of Training'. Unpublished
Thesis, London University (1948)

35 Charlton, K., Stewart, W. A. C. and Paffard, M. K.
'Students' Attitudes to Courses in Departments of Education
in Universities', *British Journal of Educational Psychology*,
28, 3 (1958)

36 Phillips, M. 'Professional Courses in the Training of
Teachers. A Report on an Enquiry into Values', Part I,
British Journal of Educational Psychology, 1, 3 (1931), 225–
45; Part II, *British Journal of Educational Psychology*, 2, 1
(1932), 1–24

37 Shipman, M. D. 'Personal and Social Influences on the
Work of a Teacher Training College'. Unpublished PhD
Thesis, London University (1965)

38 Steele, P. M. 'Changes in Attitude amongst Training College
Students towards Education in Junior Schools'. Unpublished MEd Thesis, Manchester University (1958)

39 Williams, R. H. 'Professional Studies in Teacher Training',
Education for Teaching, 61 (1963), 29–33

40 Davies, D. 'Student Teaching', in *Encyclopaedia of Educational Research*, 4th ed (Toronto, 1969)

41 Evans, K. M. 'A Study of Attitude towards Teaching as a
Career,' *British Journal of Educational Psychology*, 22, 1
(1952), 63–9

42 Evans, K. M. 'Is the Concept of "Interest" of Significance
to Success in a Teacher Training Course?', *Educational
Review*, 9 (1957), 205–11

43 Evans, K. M. 'An Examination of the Minnesota Teacher
Attitude Inventory', *British Journal of Educational Psychology*,
28, 3 (1958), 253–7

44 See note 8 this chapter

45 Ryans, D. G. *Characteristics of Teachers* (Washington, 1960)

46 Butcher, H. J. 'The Attitudes of Student Teachers to
Education: A Comparison with the Attitudes of Ex-
perienced Teachers and a Study of Changes during the
Training Course', *British Journal of Social and Clinical
Psychology*, 4 (1965), 17–24

200

47 McIntyre, D. and Morrison, A. 'The Educational Opinions of Teachers in Training', *British Journal of Social and Clinical Psychology*, 6, 1 (1967), 32–7

48 Evans, K. M. 'Teacher Training Courses and Students' Personal Qualities', *Educational Research*, 10, 1 (1967), 72–7

49 Quoted in Gage, N. L. (ed) *Handbook of Research on Teaching* (Chicago, 1963)

50 Scott, O. and Brinkley, S. G. 'Attitude Changes of Student Teachers and the Validity of the MTAI', *Journal of Educational Psychology*, 51 (1960), 76–81

51 See note 18

52 Cortis, G. A. 'Predicting Student Performance in Colleges of Education', *British Journal of Educational Psychology*, 38, 2 (1968), 115–22

53 Cortis, op cit, 117

54 Herbert, N. and Turnbull, G. H. 'Personality Factors and Effective Progress in Teaching', *Educational Review*, 16 (1963), 24–31

55 Mann, J. F. 'An Investigation into the Various Factors Influencing Success in Completing a Course in Teacher Training'. Unpublished PhD Thesis, London University (1961)

56 Warburton, F. W., Butcher, H. J. and Forrest, G. M. 'Predicting Student Performance in a University Department of Education', *British Journal of Educational Psychology* (1963), 68–79

57 Ibid, 76

58 Bowers, N. D. and Soar, R. S. 'The Influence of Teacher Personality on Classroom Interaction', *Journal of Experimental Education*, 30 (1962), 309–11

59 Evans, K. M. 'A Critical Survey of Methods of Assessing Teacher Ability', *British Journal of Educational Psychology*, 21, 2 (1951), 89–95

60 Barr, A. S. 'Wisconsin Studies of the Measurement and Prediction of Teacher Effectiveness: A Summary of Investigations', *Journal of Experimental Education*, 30 (1961) 5–156

201

61 Ibid, 150–51

62 Anderson, C. C. and Hunka, S. M. 'Teacher Evaluation', *Harvard Educational Review* Special Issue, 'Breakthrough to Better Teaching' (1968)

63 Domas, S. J. and Tiedeman, D. V. 'Teacher Competence: An Annotated Bibliography', *Journal of Experimental Education*, 19 (1950), 101–218

64 Rostker, L. E. 'The Measurement of Teaching Ability: Study Number One', *Journal of Experimental Education*, 14 (1945), 6–51

65 Rolfe, J. F. 'The Measurement of Teaching Ability: Study Number Two', *Journal of Experimental Education*, 14 (1945), 52–74

66 Cattell, R. B. 'The Assessment of Teaching Ability', *British Journal of Educational Psychology*, 1 (1931), 48–71

67 Biddle, B. J. and Ellena, W. J. (eds). *Contemporary Research on Teacher Effectiveness* (New York, 1964)

68 Cornwell, J. 'Sociometric Analysis in a Residential Training College'. Unpublished PhD Thesis, London University (1958)

69 Griffiths, A. and Moore, A. H. 'Schools and Teaching Practice', *Education for Teaching*, 73 (1967), 33–9

70 Wragg, E. C. 'Closed-circuit Television and the Training of Teachers', *Times Educational Supplement* (19 July 1968)

71 Robertson, J. D. C. 'An Analysis of the Views of Supervisors on the Attributes of Successful Graduate Student Teachers', *British Journal of Educational Psychology*, 27, 2 (1957), 115–26

72 Poppleton, P. K. 'Assessment of Teaching Practice. What Criteria do we Use?', *Education for Teaching*, 75 (1968), 59–64

73 Cohen, L. 'College and the Training of Teachers', *Educational Research*, 11, 1 (1968), 14–22

74 Finlayson, D. S. and Cohen, L. 'The Teacher's Role: A Comparative Study of the Conceptions of College of Education Students and Head Teachers', *British Journal of Educational Psychology*, 37, 1 (1967), 22–31

75 Collier, K. G. 'The Criteria of Assessment of Practical Teaching'. *Education for Teaching*, 48 (1959), 36–40

76 Joyce, B. R. and Harootunian, B. 'Teaching as Problem-solving', *Journal of Teacher Education* (December 1964)

77 McGrath, G. D. 'Some Experiences with a Student-teacher Questionnaire', *Journal of Educational Research*, 43 (1950), 641–7

78 Collier, K. G. 'The Study of Students' Attitudes', *Education for Teaching*, 42 (1957), 34–41

79 Tibble, J. W. 'Problems in the Training of Teachers and Social Workers', *Sociological Review*, Monograph no 2 (1959)

80 Baker, J. R. 'A Teacher Co-tutor Scheme', *Education for Teaching*, 73 (1967), 25–30

81 Caspari, I. and Eggleston, J. 'A New Approach to the Supervision of Teaching Practice', *Education for Teaching*, 68 (1965), 47–52

82 Clark, J. M. 'Supervision of Teaching Practice', *Education for Teaching*, 74 (1967), 44–50

83 ATCDE Education Section. *The Study of Education in Colleges of Education for Teaching* (1962)

84 National Union of Teachers. *Teacher Education – the Way Ahead* (1970)

85 Cope, E. *School Experience in Teacher Education* (Bristol, 1971)

86 Wragg, E. C. 'An Analysis of the Verbal Classroom Inter-action between Graduate Student Teachers and Children.' Unpublished PhD Thesis, Exeter University (1972)

87 Stones, E. and Morris, S. *Teaching Practice: Problems and Perspectives* (1972)

88 Price, G. 'The Crisis in School Practice', *Education for Teaching*, 65 (1964), 36–40

89 Shipman, M. D. 'Theory and Practice in the Education of Teachers', *Educational Research*, 9 (1967), 208–12

90 Collins, M. 'Untrained and Trained Graduate Teachers: A Comparison of their Experiences during the Probationary

Year', *British Journal of Educational Psychology*, 34 (1964), 75–84

91 Turner, R. L. 'Task Performance and Teaching Skill in the Intermediate Grades', *Journal of Teacher Education*, 14 (1963)

92 Clark, R. P. and Nisbet, J. D. *The First Two Years of Teaching*. Mimeographed report, Aberdeen College of Education. (1963)

93 Rudd, W. C. A. and Wiseman, S. 'Sources of Dissastisfaction among a Group of Teachers', *British Journal of Educational Psychology*, 32, 3 (1962), 275–91

94 See note 36

95 Bach, J. O. 'Practice Teaching Success in Relation to Other Measures of Teaching Ability', *Journal of Experimental Education*, 21 (1952), 57–80

96 Pearce, W. M. A Follow-up Study of Training College Students, *Education for Teaching*, 48 (1959), 41–8

97 Tudhope, W. B. 'A Study of the Training College Final Teaching Mark as a Criterion of Future Success in the Teaching Profession', Part I, *British Journal of Educational Psychology*, 12, 3 (1942), 167–71; Part II, *British Journal of Educational Psychology*, 13, 1 (1943), 16–23

98 Collins, M. 'A Follow-up Study of some Former Graduate Student Teachers', *British Journal of Educational Psychology*, 29, 3, (1959) 187–97

99 Wiseman, S. and Start, K. B. 'A Follow-up of Teachers Five Years After Completing their Training', *British Journal of Educational Psychology*, 35, 3 (1965), 342–61

100 Collins, M. *Students into Teachers* (1969)

101 Edmonds, E. L. *The First Year of Teaching* (NUT, 1966)

102 Nisbet, J. D. 'A Twenty Year Follow-up of Intelligence Test Scores', *Advancement of Science*, 41 (1954), 13–16

3: Interaction Analysis (pages 71–102)

1 Rosenshine, B. *Teaching Behaviours and Student Achievement* (Slough, 1971), 13

2 Jackson, P. W. *Life in Classrooms* (New York, 1968)
3 Joyce, B. R. and Harootunian, B., op cit
4 Wragg, op cit (1967)
5 Wragg, op cit (1972)
6 Wallen, N. E. and Travers, R. M. W. 'Analysis and Investigation of Teaching Methods', in Gage, op cit, 448–505
7 Simon, A. and Boyer, E. G. (eds) *Mirrors for Behaviour*, vols 1–6 (Philadelphia, 1968); vols 7–14, Summary, Supplementary A and B (Philadelphia, 1970)
8 Medley, D. M. and Mitzel, H. E. 'Measuring Classroom Behaviour by Systematic Observation', in Gage, op cit, 247–328
9 Anderson, H. H. 'The Measurement of Domination and of Socially Integrative Behaviour in Teachers' Contacts with Children', *Child Development*, 10 (1939), 73–89
10 Lewin, K., Lippitt, R. and White, R. K. 'Patterns of Aggressive Behaviour in Experimentally Created "Social Climates" ', *Journal of Social Psychology*, 10 (1939), 271–99
11 Withall, J. 'The Development of a Technique for the Measurement of Social-Emotional Climate in Classrooms', *Journal of Experimental Education*, 17 (1949), 347–61
12 Flanders, N. A. *Teacher Influence, Pupil Attitudes and Achievement*, US Dept of Health, Education and Welfare Cooperative Research Monograph no 12 (1965)
13 Flanders, N. A. *Analysing Teaching Behaviour* (New York, 1970)
14 Scott, W. A. 'Reliability of Content Analysis: The Case for Nominal Coding', *Public Opinion Quarterly*, 19 (1955), 321–5
15 Flanders, op cit (1970)
16 Wragg, E. C. 'A Study of Student Teachers in the Classroom', in G. Chanan (ed). *Towards a Science of Teaching* (Slough, 1973), 85–134
17 Amidon, E. J. and Hunter, E. *Improving Teaching – The Analysis of Classroom Verbal Interaction* (New York, 1966)
18 Rosenshine, op cit, 19–21
19 Galloway, C. *A Description of Teacher Behaviour: Verbal and Non-Verbal* (Columbus, Ohio, 1968)

20 Ober, R. L. *The Reciprocal Category System* (Morgantown, West Virginia, 1968)

21 Hough, J. B. 'An Observational System for the Analysis of Classroom Instruction'. Unpublished paper, Columbus, Ohio (1966)

22 Zahn, R. D. 'The Use of Interaction Analysis in Supervising Student Teachers'. Unpublished PhD Thesis, Temple University (1965)

23 Smidchens, U. and Roth, R. 'Use of a Computer in Providing Feedback to Teachers', *Classroom Interaction Newsletter*, 4, 1 (1968), 47–60

24 Wragg, E. C. 'Interaction Analysis in the Foreign Language Classroom', *Modern Language Journal* (February 1970), 116–20

25 Hough, J. B. and Amidon, E. J. 'Behavioural Change in Pre-service Teacher Preparation'. Unpublished paper, Temple University (1963)

26 Kirk, J. 'Effects of Learning the Minnesota System of Interaction Analysis by Student Teachers of Intermediate Grades'. PhD Thesis, Temple University (1964)

27 Zahn, op cit

28 Furst, N. A. 'The Effects of Training in Interaction Analysis on the Behaviour of Student Teachers in Secondary Schools', in E. J. Amidon and J. B. Hough (eds) *Interaction Analysis* (Reading, Mass, 1967)

29 Moskowitz, G. 'The Attitudes and Teaching Patterns of Cooperating Teachers and Student Teachers Trained in Interaction Analysis', in Amidon and Hough, op cit

30 Gunnison, J. P. 'An Experiment to Determine the Effects of Changing Teacher Classroom Behaviour through Training of Student Teachers in the Use of Flanders Interaction Analysis System'. PhD Thesis, Arizona State University (1968)

31 Storlie, T. R. 'Selected Characteristics of Teachers Whose Verbal Behaviour is Influenced by an In-service Course in Interaction Analysis'. PhD Thesis, University of Minnesota (1961)

32 Withall, J. and Fagan, E. R. 'The Effects of an NOEA Course on the Contacts and Verbal Behaviour used by English and Reading Teachers to Instruct Disadvantaged Youth', *Classroom Interaction Newsletter*, 2, 1 (1966), 15–19

33 Morgan, J. C. 'A Study of the Observed Behaviour of Student Teachers in Secondary Social Studies as Correlates with Certain Personality Characteristics and Creativity', *Classroom Interaction Newsletter*, 2, 2 (1967), 34–5

34 Schueler, H., Gold, M. J. and Mitzel, H. E. *The Use of Television for Improving Teacher Training and for Improving Measures of Student-teaching Performance* (New York, 1962)

35 Wragg, op cit (1972)

36 As did Jackson, op cit (1968). See note 2 of this chapter

37 Simon and Boyer, op cit (1968 and 1970). See note 7 of this chapter

38 Simon and Boyer, op cit (1968), vol 2

39 Ibid

40 Ibid

41 Ibid

42 Ibid, vol 3

43 Ibid

44 Ibid, vol 5

45 Simon and Boyer, op cit (1970), vol 7

46 Ibid, vol 8

47 Ibid

48 Ibid

49 Ibid, vol 12

50 Ibid, vol 7

51 Ibid, vol 11

52 Ibid, op cit Supplementary vol A

53 Ibid, vol 11

54 Simon and Boyer, op cit, (1968), vol 5

55 Ibid, vol 3

56 Simon and Boyer, op cit (1970), vol 13

57 Grittner, F. M. *Teaching Foreign Languages* (New York, 1969)

58 Simon and Boyer, op cit (1970), vol 8

59 Simon and Boyer, op cit (1968), vol 3

60 Simon and Boyer, op cit (1970), vol 10
61 Ibid
62 Evans, D. and Wragg, E. C. 'The Use of a Verbal Interaction Technique with Severely Subnormal Children', *Journal of Mental Subnormality* (December 1969)
63 Simon and Boyer, op cit (1970), vol 7
64 Simon and Boyer, op cit (1968), vol 5
65 Simon and Boyer, op cit (1970), Supplementary vol A
66 Ibid, vol 9

4: Micro-teaching (pages 103–36)

1 Stanford University. *Micro-teaching: A Description* (Stanford, 1968)
2 Allen, D. and Ryan, K. *Micro-teaching* (Reading, Mass, 1969)
3 Borg, W. R., Kelley, M. J., Langer, P. and Gall, M. *The Mini Course: A Microteaching Approach to Teacher Education* (1970)
4 Stones and Morris, op cit, 79–101
5 Bandura, A. and Walters, R. *Social Learning and Personality Development* (New York, 1963)
6 McAleese, W. R. and Unwin, D. 'Microteaching: A Selective Survey', *Programmed Learning and Educational Technology*, 8, 1 (1971)
7 Allen and Ryan, op cit, 15–23
8 Ward, B. E. *A Survey of Microteaching in N.C.A.T.E. Accredited Secondary Education Programs* (Stanford, 1970)
9 Taba, H., Levine, S. and Elzey, F. *Thinking in Elementary School Children* (Washington, 1964)
10 Johnson, W. 'Doctoral Dissertation', Stanford University (1964). Quoted in Allen and Ryan, op cit, 20
11 Hovland, C. I. (ed). *The Order of Presentation in Persuasion* (New Haven, Conn, 1957)
12 Horner, M. *Movement, Voice and Speech* (1970)
13 Ward, I. C. *The Phonetics of English* (Cambridge, 1962)

14 Fishman, M. *The Actor in Training* (1961)
15 Grotowski, J. *Towards a Poor Theatre* (1969)
16 Allen and Ryan, op cit, 49
17 Perrott, E. and Duthie, J. H. 'Television as a Feedback Device: Microteaching', *Educational Television International*, 4, 4 (1970), 258–61
18 Thorndike, E. L. *Human Learning* (1931, reprinted Harvard, Mass, 1966)
19 Pressey, S. L. 'A Simple Apparatus which gives Test Scores – and Teaches', *School and Society*, 23 (1926), 373–6
20 Skinner, B. F. *Science and Human Behaviour* (New York, 1953)
21 Bruner, J. S., Goodman, J. J. and Austin, G. A. *A Study of Thinking* (New York, 1956)
22 Annett, J. *Feedback and Human Behaviour* (1969)
23 Lewin, K. 'Psychology and the Process of Group Living', *Journal of Social Psychology*, 17 (1943), 113–31
24 Domas and Tiedeman, op cit
25 Johnson, W. D. and Knaupp, K. E. 'Trainee Role Expectations of the Microteaching Supervisor', *Journal of Teacher Education*, 21, 3 (1970), 396–401
26 Stones and Morris, op cit, 92
27 Caspari and Eggleston, op cit
28 Belt, W. D. and Baird, J. H. 'Micro-teaching in the Training of Teachers', in *Progress and Problems. Multi-State Teacher Education Project* (Baltimore, 1967), 20–22
29 Britton, R. J. and Leith, G. O. M. 'An Experimental Evaluation of the Effects of Microteaching on Teaching Performance'. Mimeo, University of Sussex (Brighton, 1971)
30 Trott, A. 'Microteaching: An Examination'. Mimeo, Berkshire College of Education (Reading, 1972)
31 Borg et al, op cit
32 Hutchins, C. L., Dunning, B., Madsen, M. and Rainey, S. I. *Minicourses Work* (Berkeley, 1971)
33 Ward, B. A., Masla, J. A., Licita, W., Pankratz, R. S., Mook, J. and Smith, W. *The Minicourse in Teacher Education* (Berkeley, 1972)

34 Hutchins et al, op cit, 19–21
35 Ibid, 75
36 Ward et al, op cit (1972), 28
37 Ward, B. E., op cit
38 Koran, J. J. 'Supervision: An Attempt to Modify Behaviour', *Educational Leadership*, 26 (1969)
39 Stewig, J. W. 'What Should College Supervisors Do?', *Journal of Teacher Education*, 21, 2 (1970), 251–7
40 Olivero, J. H. *Microteaching: Medium for Improving Instruction* (Merrill, Ohio, 1970)
41 Wragg, E. C. 'The Influence of Feedback on Teachers' Performance', *Educational Research*, 13, 3 (1971), 218–21

5: *Simulation and Role-playing* (*pages* 137–59)

1 Taylor, J. L. and Walford, R. *Simulation in the Classroom* (1972)
2 Moreno, J. *The Theatre of Spontaneity* (1947)
3 Klein, J. *Working with Groups* (1964)
4 Tansey, P. J. (ed). *Educational Aspects of Simulation* (1971)
5 Tansey, P. J. and Unwin, D. *Simulation and Gaming in Education* (1969)
6 Stones and Morris, op cit, 70–78
7 Kersch, B. Y. 'The Classroom Simulator', *Journal of Teacher Education*, 13 (1962), 109–10
8 Cruickshank, D. R., Broadbent, F. W. and Bubb, R. L. *Teaching Problems Laboratory* (Chicago, 1967)
9 Adelman, C. and Walker, R. 'Communication Games'. Mimeo, Chelsea College, Centre for Science Education (1972)
10 Argyle, M. *The Psychology of Interpersonal Behaviour* (1967)
11 Smith, L. M. and Geoffrey, W. *The Complexities of the Urban Classroom* (New York, 1968)
12 Cage, J. *Silence* (1961)
13 Rogers, C. *Freedom to Learn* (New York, 1969)
14 Amidon, E. J. 'Project on Student Teaching'. Mimeo, Temple University, Philadelphia (1967)

15 Corsini, R. J. and Howard, D. D. (eds) *Critical Incidents in Teaching* (New Jersey, 1964)

16 Flanagan, J. C. 'Critical Requirements: A New Approach to Employee Evaluation', *Personnel Psychology*, 2 (1949), 419–25

17 Ryans, D. G. *Characteristics of Teachers* (Washington, 1960)

18 Kounin, J. S. and Gump, P. V. 'The Ripple Effect in Discipline', *Elementary School Journal*, 59 (1958), 158–62

19 Haysom, J. and Sutton, C. *Science Teacher Education Project, Trial of Curriculum Units* (1972)

20 Start, K. B. and Wells, B. K. *The Trend of Reading Standards* (Slough, 1972)

21 Torrance, E. P. *Guiding Creative Talent* (Englewood Cliffs, NJ, 1962)

22 Mooney, R. L. 'Creation in the Classroom Setting', in R. L. Mooney and T. A. Razik. *Explorations in Creativity* (New York, 1967), 206–15

23 Getzels, J. W. and Jackson, P. W. *Creativity and Intelligence: Explorations with Gifted Students* (New York, 1962)

24 Cropley, A. J. *Creativity* (1967)

25 Parnes, S. J. and Meadow, A. 'Effects of Brainstorming Instructions on Creative Problem-solving by Trained and Untrained Subjects', *Journal of Educational Psychology*, 50 (1959), 171–6

26 Parnes, S. J. and Meadow, A. 'Evaluation of Persistence of Effects Produced by a Creative Problem-solving Course', *Psychological Reports*, 7 (1960), 357–61

27 For example, the Schools Council Research and Development Project in Compensatory Education based at University College, Swansea, or their 'Scope' kits for teaching immigrant children.

28 Including use of materials such as the Peabody Language Development Kit produced by the American Guidance Service (1965)

29 Such as described by W. M. Possien, in *They All Need to Talk* (New York, 1969)

30 Goldman, R. J. 'Creative Methods in the Education of Teachers', *Education for Teaching* (November 1966), 5–10

6: *Teaching Practice and Work with Children* (*pages* 160–84)

1 Pedley, R. 'Teaching Practice', in Exeter University Institute of Education. *Themes in Education*, no 19 (1969), 5
2 Cope, E. *School Experience in Teacher Education* (Bristol, 1971)
3 Pedley, op cit, 6
4 Department of Education and Science. *Teacher Education and Training* (1972)
5 Otty, N. *Learner Teacher* (1972), 19
6 Brimer, M. A. and Dunn, L. M. *The English Picture Vocabulary Tests* (Bristol, 1962)
7 Kirk, S. A. and Kirk, W. D. *Psycholinguistic Learning Disabilities: Diagnosis and Remediation* (Urbana, 1971)
8 Downes, L. W. and Shaw, K. E. 'Study Practice in St Luke's College, Exeter', in Exeter University. *Themes in Education*, op cit, 15–17
9 Johnson Abercrombie, M. L. *The Anatomy of Human Judgment* (1960), 142
10 Stones and Morris, op cit, 7
11 Cohen, A. and Garner, N. *A Student's Guide to Teaching Practice* (1971), 14
12 Grant, J. J. 'A "Social Practice" in the Training of Teachers: A West German Model', *Education for Teaching* (Autumn, 1967), 19–24
13 Central Advisory Council for Education (England). *Children and Their Primary Schools* (1967)
14 Midwinter, E. *Priority Education* (1972)
15 Ibid, 71
16 Hannam, C., Smyth, P. and Stephenson, N. *Young Teachers and Reluctant Learners* (1971)
17 Ibid, 109

7: *Resources* (*pages* 185–94)

1 Taylor, L. C. *Resources for Learning* (1971)
2 Wittich, W. A. and Schuller, C. F. *Audiovisual Materials* (New York, 1967)

3   Moreman, K. 'Time-lapse Techniques in Cinematography', in P. D. Groves (ed). *Film in Higher Education and Research* (Oxford, 1966), 197–208
4   Chubb, J. C. 'Film as a Teaching Aid', in Groves, op cit, 95–123
5   Groves, op cit
6   Duncan, C. J. 'The Role of the Producer of Academic Films' in Groves, op cit, 211–41
7   Lucey, E. 'Who Can Afford a Film?', in Groves, op cit, 243–75
8   Gardener, C. G. 'An Amateur's Approach to Film Making', in Groves, op cit (1966), 303–11
9   UNESCO Division of Methods, Materials and Techniques. *Closed Circuit Television Equipment for Use in Training: Technical Dossier.* Mimeo (Paris, 1972)
10 Peck, R. F. and Tucker, J. A. 'Research on Teacher Education' in R. M. W. Travers (ed). *Second Handbook of Research on Teaching* (Chicago, 1973), 970

Appendix A

What is encouraging about recent developments in Britain and elsewhere in the field of teacher education is that the concept of a single spell of training for a lifetime in the profession has been challenged. If the appetite for in-service education is to be increased and sustained, then people and resources are of prime importance. The foregoing chapters have described many kinds of activity which can be initiated by a tutor in a college, but increasingly school personnel are being involved, to the considerable professional enrichment of all concerned. I close with brief notes about teacher tutors, professional tutors and a plea for regional and national resources centres.

Teacher tutors

In many countries for a number of years practising teachers have been associated with students on teaching practice like master and apprentice. It was the basis of early teacher training as described in Chapter 1. In the United States the teacher might be designated cooperating teacher, and he might receive a fee or be allowed free in-service courses at the institution he was serving.

In Britain teacher tutor schemes have been operated recently by Leicester University and a number of other universities and colleges. The advantages where the scheme works well are that the student gets on-the-spot help from a practitioner in the school; the teacher tutor can ease the transition from college to school by pastoral care, particularly in the early stages of teaching practice; the teacher tutor is normally a competent teacher himself, often with the class or in the subject concerned, and therefore offers both insights into difficulties and his own teaching style as an additional model for the student to see; finally the act of supervising a student usually compels him to reappraise his own teaching and stay abreast of current developments, and in this respect a useful in-service function is performed.

The links between college and school can be strengthened when teacher tutors assemble in the college for briefing sessions or meet students for discussions, and when college tutors take their classes. It is not unknown for a regular exchange of this nature to take place, whereby the tutor fills in for the teacher, say every Tuesday afternoon, while the latter spends his time with students. Similarly the teacher tutor can play an important part in study practice, as described in Chapter 6.

Professional tutors

The James Report (1971) recommended that the teacher tutor role as described above should be extended and expanded.

> Every school should have on its staff a 'professional tutor' to coordinate second and third cycle work affecting the school and be the link between the school and other agencies engaged in that work ... Among the responsibilities of the professional tutor would be that of compiling and maintaining a training programme for the staff of the school, which would take account both of the curricular needs of the school and the professional needs of the teachers.[1]

In larger schools the professional tutor might coordinate a team of perhaps six or eight teacher tutors as well as take general responsibility for students and probationer teachers himself.

Gibson[2] has edited a collection of contributions about the wide and important responsibilities of this new school-based organiser and coordinator of teacher education and training, who is clearly going to play an important part in the future. With his unique position inside the school if the proposals are applied as they were framed, he will be in a strong position to influence and stimulate the appetite for further training in the profession.

Resources centres

It is now a matter of the greatest urgency that both nationally

215

and regionally resources should be pooled. In the previous chapter there was considerable mention of the advantages of cooperatives. The Science Teacher Education Programme referred to in Chapter 5 was a fine example of the gathering together of high quality materials and good ideas by teams of people.

It in no way suppresses individual initiative to allow access to pooled facilities. Indeed it amplifies it. There is urgent need for a wide variety of films of classrooms and teachers of all kinds. Until considerable finance is made available, most institutions will make their own on a limited budget. On the whole this is extremely healthy, and home-made materials are often the backbone of a training course, producing a high level of commitment and interest among those who have produced them. National and Regional Resources Centres could both support and amplify these local initiatives, as well as provide machinery for exchange between institutions that have shared interests.

1   James Report (1971), section 2, 25
2   Gibson, R. (ed). *The Professional Tutor* (Cambridge, 1972)

Appendix B

ESTIMATED COST OF TELEVISION EQUIPMENT MODULES

It is impossible to give firm prices for equipment as these change rapidly within a relatively short period of time. In the UNESCO Conference Report (Chapter 7, note 9) the cost of various modules is based on 1972 dollar prices. These are as follows:

Module I   Transmission unit
For three classrooms, each equipped with two 23 in monitors, the cost is estimated at $3,500. This allows for two VTR machines, a demodulator, a VT monitor, six 23 in monitors and stands, and other small items. There would be an annual recurrent cost of up to approximately $750 for maintenance and tape renewal.

Module II   Observation unit
Mains equipment consisting of camera, VTR, gun microphone fixed to camera, two hypercardioid microphones, one neck microphone, stands, 800W quartz iodine lamp, sound mixer and other small accessories, plus fifty videotapes is costed at $3,250. Portable equipment similar to the above would be $2,750. A combined Module I and Module II suitable for 150 trainees is estimated at $6,750.

Module III   Reporting and production studio
The capital cost of such a studio would range from $22,000 to $35,000, which includes $3,500 for a vehicle and $4,250 for fifty 1 in and fifty ½-inch tapes. The recurrent costs are $3,000 for maintenance and $4,000 for renewal of tapes, replacement of bulbs, lamps etc. This excludes the cost of a full-time technician or tutor, both of which are essential.

217

Module IV   A production centre
No details of cost are given, as these would obviously vary from country to country and region to region, but the cost might well be in excess of $100,000, with substantial annual salary, maintenance and replacement requirements.

Select Bibliography

Allen, D., and Ryan, K. *Micro-teaching* (Reading, Mass, 1969)

Biddle, B. J. and Ellena, W. J. (eds). *Contemporary Research on Teacher Effectiveness* (New York, 1964)

Collins, M. *Students into Teachers* (1969)

Cope, E. *School Experience in Teacher Education* (Bristol, 1971)

Flanders, N. L. *Analysing Teacher Behaviour* (New York, 1970)

Gage, N. L. *Handbook of Research on Teaching* (Chicago, 1963)

Hannam, C., Smyth, P. and Stephenson, N. *Young Teachers and Reluctant Learners* (1971)

Hilsum, S. and Cane, B. S. *The Teacher's Day* (Sough, 1971)

Rich, R. W. *The Training of Teachers in England and Wales during the Nineteenth Century* (Cambridge, 1933)

Simon, A. and Boyer, E. G. (eds). *Mirrors for Behaviour* (Philadelphia, 1968 and 1970)

Stones, E. and Morris, S. *Teaching Practice: Problems and Perspective* (1972)

Tansey, P. J. (ed). *Educational Aspects of Simulation* (1971)

Taylor, L. C. *Resources for Learning* (1971)

Taylor, W. *Towards a Policy for the Education of Teachers* (Bristol, 1969)

Travers, R. M. W. *Second Handbook of Research on Teaching* (Chicago, 1973)

Acknowledgements

To my former colleagues David Evans, Tony Edwards, Bryan Stephenson, Geoffrey Fox and Dick Tahta of Exeter University School of Education for the stimulus of constant discussion, though each might wish to disagree with all or part of this book, and to Peter Hill for considerable help with historical sources.

To Professor Dick D'Aeth, Head of the School of Education at Exeter University, who allowed and encouraged us to innovate.

To Ned Flanders and Anita Simon, inexhaustibly helpful friends in the USA.

To the enthusiastic teachers who lent us children, ideas, materials and themselves.

To the many long-suffering groups of students with whom it is a pleasure to work, and whose interest and integrity reassure me about the future of the profession.

To Lily Douglas, who not only deciphered my handwriting but typed the manuscript.

E.C.W.

Index

Froebel, 41
Fuller, F., 38, 195, 197
Furst, N. A., 94, 206

Gage, N. L., 201
Galloway, C., 81, 205
Garner, N., 174, 212
Getzels, J. W., 157, 211
Gibson, R., 215, 216
Goldman, R. J., 159, 211
Grant, J. J., 51, 174, 199, 212
Griffiths, A., 61, 202
Grittner, F. M., 100, 207
Grotowski, J., 118, 208
Groves, P. D., 189–90, 213
Gump, P. V., 150, 211
Gunnison, J. P., 95, 206

Halliwell, K., 49, 199
Hannam, C., 51, 176, 199, 212
Harootunian, B., 63, 72, 203, 205
Herbert, J., 101–2
Herbert, N., 56, 201
Hillview project, 175–6
Hilsum, S., viii, 195
Holmes, B., 23, 196
Holt, John, 41
Honigman system, 98
Horace, M., 27, 196
Horner, M., 118, 208
Hough, J. B., 81, 94, 98, 206
Hovland, C. I., 118, 208
Howard, D. D., 148, 211
Hunka, S. M., 60, 202
Hunter, E., 80, 98, 205

In-basket technique, 150–6
Individual child study, 100–1, 163–6
Induction year, *see* Probationary year
In-service training, 19, 95–6, 132–5
Interaction analysis, 71–102, 129–30
Isaac, J., 47, 198

Jackson, P. W., 72, 157, 205, 207, 211

224

226